TABLE OF CONTENTS

DOWN-HOME DELIGHTS

Pork and Corn Bread Stuffing Casserole

¹/₂ teaspoon paprika
¹/₄ teaspoon salt
¹/₄ teaspoon garlic powder
¹/₄ teaspoon black pepper
4 bone-in pork chops (about 1³/₄ pounds)
2 tablespoons butter
1¹/₂ cups chopped onions
³/₄ cup thinly sliced celery
³/₄ cup matchstick carrots*
¹/₄ cup chopped fresh Italian parsley
1 can (about 14 ounces) chicken broth
4 cups corn bread stuffing mix

Matchstick carrots (sometimes called shredded carrots) can be found near other prepared vegetables in the supermarket produce section.

1. Preheat oven to 350°F. Lightly coat 13×9-inch baking dish with nonstick cooking spray.

2. Combine paprika, salt, garlic powder and pepper in small bowl. Season both sides of pork chops with paprika mixture.

3. Melt butter in large skillet over medium-high heat. Add pork chops; cook 4 minutes or just until browned, turning once. Transfer to plate; set aside.

4. Add onions, celery, carrots and parsley to skillet. Cook and stir 4 minutes or until onions are translucent. Add broth; bring to a boil. Remove from heat; add stuffing mix and fluff with fork.

5. Transfer stuffing mixture to prepared baking dish. Top with pork chops. Cover; bake 25 minutes or until pork is barely pink in center. *Makes 4 servings*

Homestyle Chicken & Biscuits

1 can (10¾ ounces) CAMPBELL'S® Condensed Cream of Chicken Soup (Regular or 98% Fat Free)

¼ cup milk

¾ cup shredded Cheddar cheese

¼ teaspoon ground black pepper

1 bag (16 ounces) frozen vegetable combination (broccoli, cauliflower, carrots), thawed

2 cans (4.5 ounces each) SWANSON® Premium Chunk Chicken Breast in Water, drained

1 package (7.5 ounces) refrigerated biscuits (10 biscuits)

1. Heat the oven to 400°F. Stir the soup, milk, cheese and black pepper in a 3-quart shallow baking dish. Stir in the vegetables and chicken.

2. Bake for 15 minutes or until the chicken mixture is hot and bubbling. Stir the chicken mixture.

3. Top the chicken mixture with the biscuits. Bake for 15 minutes or until the biscuits are golden brown. *Makes 4 servings*

Kitchen Tip: Use the downtime while this one-dish meal is in the oven to make a fresh tomato salad. Slice some tomatoes and drizzle them with balsamic vinegar and olive oil.

Broccoli Casserole

2 packages (10 ounces each) frozen chopped broccoli

1 container (16 ounces) cottage cheese

1½ cups (6 ounces) grated Cheddar cheese

4 eggs, lightly beaten

6 tablespoons (¾ stick) butter, melted and cooled

Salt and black pepper

1. Preheat oven to 350°F. Cook broccoli according to package directions; drain well.

2. Mix broccoli, cottage cheese, Cheddar cheese, eggs and butter in large bowl. Season with salt and pepper. Transfer to 2-quart casserole.

3. Bake 40 minutes or until eggs are set and casserole is heated through. *Makes 4 servings*

Classic Macaroni and Cheese

   3 tablespoons butter or margarine
¼ cup finely chopped onion (optional)
   2 tablespoons all-purpose flour
½ teaspoon salt
⅛ teaspoon black pepper
   2 cups milk
   2 cups (8 ounces) SARGENTO® Fancy Shredded Mild Cheddar Cheese, divided
   2 cups elbow macaroni, cooked and drained

Melt butter in medium saucepan over medium heat. Cook onion, if desired, in butter 5 minutes or until tender. Stir in flour, salt and pepper. Gradually add milk and cook, stirring occasionally, until thickened.

Remove from heat. Add 1½ cups cheese and stir until cheese is melted. Combine cheese sauce with cooked macaroni. Place in 1½-quart casserole; top with remaining cheese. Bake in preheated 350°F oven 30 minutes or until bubbly and cheese is lightly browned.

Makes 6 servings

Turkey and Mushroom Wild Rice Casserole

   2 tablespoons butter
   1 cup sliced button mushrooms *or* 1 can (4 ounces) sliced mushrooms
   1 onion, chopped
   1 stalk celery, chopped
   2 cups diced cooked turkey breast
   1 can (10¾ ounces) condensed cream of mushroom soup, undiluted
   1 pouch (about 9 ounces) ready-to-serve wild rice
   1 cup milk
   2 tablespoons minced fresh chives
¼ teaspoon black pepper
½ cup chopped pecans

1. Preheat oven to 350°F. Melt butter in large nonstick skillet over medium heat. Add mushrooms, onion and celery; cook and stir 5 minutes or until onion is translucent. Stir in turkey, soup, wild rice, milk, chives and pepper; mix well.

2. Spoon mixture into 2-quart baking dish. Sprinkle with pecans. Bake 15 to 18 minutes or until hot and bubbly.

Makes 4 servings

Classic Macaroni and Cheese

Potato Sausage Casserole

> **1 pound** bulk pork sausage or ground pork
> **1 can (10³⁄₄ ounces)** condensed cream of mushroom soup, undiluted
> **³⁄₄ cup** milk
> **¹⁄₂ cup** chopped onion
> **¹⁄₂ teaspoon** salt
> **¹⁄₄ teaspoon** black pepper
> **3 cups** sliced potatoes
> **1 tablespoon** butter, cut into small pieces
> **1¹⁄₂ cups (6 ounces)** shredded Cheddar cheese
> Sliced green onions (optional)

1. Preheat oven to 350°F. Lightly coat 1¹⁄₂-quart casserole with nonstick cooking spray.

2. Brown sausage in large skillet over medium-high heat 6 to 8 minutes, stirring to break up meat. Drain fat.

3. Stir together soup, milk, onion, salt and pepper in medium bowl.

4. Place half of potatoes in prepared casserole. Top with half of soup mixture; sprinkle with half of sausage. Repeat layers, ending with sausage. Dot with butter.

5. Cover casserole with foil. Bake 1¹⁄₄ to 1¹⁄₂ hours or until potatoes are tender. Uncover; sprinkle with cheese. Bake until cheese is melted and casserole is bubbly. Garnish with green onions.　　　　　　　　　　　　　　　　　　　　　　　　　　　*Makes 4 to 6 servings*

Tip Always choose firm, relatively smooth, clean potatoes. Potatoes should be reasonably well-shaped and free from cuts or bruises. Avoid green-colored potatoes and those with sprouts.

Seafood Pot Pie

½ of a 17.3-ounce package PEPPERIDGE FARM® Puff Pastry Sheets (1 sheet)
Vegetable cooking spray
1 can (10¾ ounces) CAMPBELL'S® Condensed Cream of Onion Soup
1 can (10¾ ounces) CAMPBELL'S® Condensed New England Clam Chowder
½ cup milk
⅛ teaspoon hot pepper sauce
1 package (10 ounces) frozen mixed vegetables, thawed
1 bag (12 ounces) frozen cooked baby shrimp, thawed (about 3 cups)
1 can (about 6 ounces) imitation crabmeat (surimi)

1. Thaw the pastry at room temperature for 40 minutes or until it's easy to handle. Heat the oven to 375°F. Spray a 12×8×2-inch shallow baking dish with cooking spray.

2. Stir the soups, milk, hot sauce, vegetables, shrimp and crabmeat into the prepared dish.

3. Unfold the pastry sheet on a lightly floured surface. Roll the sheet into a 10×9-inch rectangle. Gently roll the pastry onto the rolling pin so that you can lift it and gently unroll it on the baking dish. Crimp or roll the edges to seal it to the dish.

4. Bake for 40 minutes or until the pastry is golden brown and the filling is hot and bubbling. Let the pot pie stand for 5 minutes before serving. *Makes 4 servings*

Honey-Baked Heaven

8 large Granny Smith apples, peeled and sliced
2 packages (8 ounces each) kielbasa sausage, cut into ½-inch slices
1⅓ cups honey
¼ cup water
1 tablespoon ground cinnamon
⅓ cup butter, cubed

1. Preheat oven to 350°F. Grease 13×9-inch baking dish.

2. Arrange apples and sausage in prepared baking dish.

3. Combine honey, water and cinnamon in medium bowl; mix well. Pour over apples and sausage. Dot with butter.

4. Bake 40 minutes or until apples are softened, basting with pan juices occasionally.
Makes 6 to 8 servings

Seafood Pot Pie

Home-Style Shepherd's Pie

½ pound ground beef
½ pound mild Italian sausage, casings removed
1 cup chopped onion
2 cups frozen mixed vegetables, thawed
1 cup water
1 can (6 ounces) tomato paste
¼ cup chopped fresh Italian parsley
1 tablespoon beef bouillon granules
2 teaspoons sugar
¼ teaspoon salt
¼ teaspoon black pepper
⅛ teaspoon ground red pepper
1 package (2 pounds) refrigerated mashed potatoes
1½ cups (6 ounces) shredded sharp Cheddar cheese
½ cup chopped green onions

1. Preheat oven to 350°F. Lightly coat 12×8-inch baking dish with nonstick cooking spray.

2. Brown beef and sausage in large nonstick skillet over medium-high heat 6 to 8 minutes, stirring to break up meat. Drain all but 1 tablespoon fat. Add onion; cook and stir 2 minutes or until translucent. Add vegetables, water, tomato paste, parsley, bouillon, sugar, salt, black pepper and red pepper; stir until well blended.

3. Transfer mixture to prepared baking dish. Spoon potatoes evenly over mixture. Sprinkle with cheese and green onions. Coat sheet of foil with cooking spray. Cover dish with foil, sprayed side down. Bake 22 to 25 minutes or until hot and bubbly. *Makes 8 servings*

Turkey Apple Cranberry Bake

> 1 cup PEPPERIDGE FARM® Herb Seasoned Stuffing
> 1 tablespoon butter, melted
> 1 can (10¾ ounces) CAMPBELL'S® Condensed Cream of Celery Soup (Regular or 98% Fat Free)
> ½ cup milk
> 2 cups cubed cooked turkey
> 1 medium apple, diced (about 1½ cups)
> 1 stalk celery, finely chopped (about ½ cup)
> ½ cup dried cranberries
> ½ cup pecan halves, chopped

1. Stir the stuffing and butter in a small bowl. Set aside.

2. Stir the soup, milk, turkey, apple, celery, cranberries and pecans in a 12×8×2-inch shallow baking dish. Sprinkle the reserved stuffing mixture over the turkey mixture.

3. Bake at 400°F. for 30 minutes or until hot and bubbly.   *Makes 4 servings*

Hearty Beef and Potato Casserole

> 1 package (about 17 ounces) refrigerated fully cooked beef pot roast in gravy*
> 3 cups frozen hash brown potatoes, divided
> ¼ teaspoon *each* salt and black pepper
> 1 can (about 14 ounces) diced tomatoes
> ½ cup canned chipotle chile sauce
> 1 cup (4 ounces) shredded sharp Cheddar cheese

*Fully cooked beef pot roast in gravy can be found in the refrigerated prepared meats section of the supermarket.

1. Preheat oven to 375°F. Lightly coat 11×7-inch baking dish with nonstick cooking spray.

2. Drain and discard gravy from pot roast. Cut beef into ¼-inch-thick slices. Place 2 cups potatoes in prepared baking dish. Sprinkle with salt and pepper. Top with beef. Combine tomatoes and chile sauce in small bowl; spread evenly over beef. Top with remaining 1 cup potatoes. Sprinkle with cheese.

3. Lightly cover dish with foil. Bake 20 minutes. Remove foil; bake 20 minutes or until hot and bubbly. Let stand 5 to 10 minutes before serving.   *Makes 6 servings*

Turkey Apple Cranberry Bake

Company Crab

    1 pound Florida blue crabmeat, fresh, frozen or pasteurized
    1 can (15 ounces) artichoke hearts, drained
    1 can (4 ounces) sliced mushrooms, drained
    2 tablespoons butter or margarine
 2¹⁄₂ tablespoons all-purpose flour
  ¹⁄₂ teaspoon salt
  ¹⁄₈ teaspoon ground red pepper
    1 cup half-and-half
    2 tablespoons dry sherry
    2 tablespoons crushed cornflakes
    1 tablespoon grated Parmesan cheese
      Paprika

Preheat oven to 450°F. Thaw crabmeat if frozen. Remove any pieces of shell or cartilage. Cut artichoke hearts in half; place artichokes in well-greased, shallow 1¹⁄₂-quart casserole. Add crabmeat and mushrooms; cover and set aside.

Melt butter in small saucepan over medium heat. Stir in flour, salt and ground red pepper. Gradually stir in half-and-half. Continue cooking until sauce thickens, stirring constantly. Stir in sherry. Pour sauce over crabmeat. Combine cornflakes and cheese in small bowl; sprinkle over casserole. Sprinkle with paprika. Bake 12 to 15 minutes or until bubbly.   *Makes 6 servings*

Favorite recipe from *Florida Department of Agriculture and Consumer Services, Bureau of Seafood and Aquaculture*

Tip Pasteurized crabmeat has been heat treated and sealed in an airtight container. It stays fresh significantly longer than unpasteurized crabmeat as long as it is unopened and refrigerated. Once opened, the crabmeat should be used within 3 days.

Southern Turkey Cornbread Pot Pie

1 can (10¾ ounces) CAMPBELL'S® Condensed Cream of Chicken Soup (Regular or 98% Fat Free)
⅛ teaspoon ground black pepper
2 cups cubed cooked turkey
1 can (about 8 ounces) whole kernel corn, drained
1 package (11 ounces) refrigerated cornbread twists

1. Heat the oven to 425°F.

2. Heat the soup, black pepper, turkey and corn in a 2-quart saucepan over medium heat until the mixture is hot and bubbling. Pour the turkey mixture into a 9-inch pie plate.

3. Separate the cornbread into **8** pieces along perforations. (Do not unroll dough.) Place over the hot turkey mixture. Bake for 15 minutes or until the bread is golden.   *Makes 4 servings*

Easy Substitution Tip: Substitute cooked chicken for the turkey.

Prep Time: 5 minutes
Cook Time: 5 minutes
Bake Time: 15 minutes

Sweet and Savory Sausage Casserole

2 sweet potatoes, peeled and cut into 1-inch cubes
2 apples, peeled, cored and cut into 1-inch cubes
1 onion, cut into thin strips
2 tablespoons vegetable oil
2 teaspoons Italian seasoning
1 teaspoon garlic powder
½ teaspoon *each* salt and black pepper
1 pound cooked Italian sausage, cut into ½-inch pieces

1. Preheat oven to 400°F. Lightly coat 13×9-inch baking dish with nonstick cooking spray.

2. Combine sweet potatoes, apples, onion, oil, seasoning, garlic powder, salt and pepper in large bowl. Toss to coat evenly. Transfer to prepared baking dish.

3. Cover; bake 30 minutes. Add sausage; bake 10 minutes or until sausage is heated through and sweet potatoes are tender.   *Makes 4 to 6 servings*

Southern Turkey Cornbread Pot Pie

Chicken and Wild Rice Casserole

    2 slices bacon, chopped
    3 tablespoons olive oil
1½ pounds chicken thighs
     Salt and black pepper
  ½ cup diced onion
  ½ cup diced celery
    2 tablespoons Worcestershire sauce
  ½ teaspoon dried sage
   1 cup converted long grain white rice
   1 package (4 ounces) wild rice
   6 ounces cremini mushrooms, quartered
   3 cups hot chicken broth, or enough to cover chicken
   2 tablespoons chopped fresh Italian parsley

Slow Cooker Directions

1. Microwave bacon on HIGH 1 minute. Transfer to slow cooker. Add oil and spread evenly on bottom. Place chicken in slow cooker, skin side down. Season with salt and pepper.

2. Add onion, celery, Worcestershire sauce and sage. Top with white rice, wild rice and mushrooms. Pour broth over top. Cover; cook on LOW 3 to 4 hours or until rice is tender.

3. Uncover and let stand 15 minutes. Remove skin before serving, if desired. Sprinkle with parsley. *Makes 4 to 6 servings*

Prep Time: 15 minutes
Cook Time: 3 to 4 hours

Chicken and Wild Rice Casserole

Spinach-Potato Bake

   1 pound ground beef
   1 onion, chopped
  ½ cup sliced mushrooms
   2 cloves garlic, minced
   1 package (10 ounces) frozen chopped spinach, thawed and squeezed dry
  ½ teaspoon ground nutmeg
   1 pound russet potatoes, peeled, cooked and mashed
  ¼ cup sour cream
  ¼ cup milk
     Salt and black pepper
  ½ cup (2 ounces) shredded Cheddar cheese

1. Preheat oven to 400°F. Lightly coat 9-inch square baking dish with nonstick cooking spray.

2. Brown beef in large nonstick skillet over medium-high heat 6 to 8 minutes, stirring to break up meat. Drain all but 1 tablespoon fat. Add onion, mushrooms and garlic; cook and stir until tender. Stir in spinach and nutmeg. Cook until heated through, stirring occasionally.

3. Combine potatoes, sour cream and milk. Add to beef mixture; season with salt and pepper. Spoon into prepared baking dish; sprinkle with cheese.

4. Bake 15 to 20 minutes or until slightly puffed and cheese is melted.   *Makes 6 servings*

Salmon Veg•All® Pasta Bake

   3 cups cooked small shell pasta
   1 can (15 ounces) VEG•ALL® Original Mixed Vegetables, drained
   1 can (14¾ ounces) pink salmon, drained, *or* 1 pound cooked salmon
   1 can (10¾ ounces) condensed cream of mushroom soup
  ¼ teaspoon black pepper
  ½ cup dry bread crumbs

Preheat oven to 350°F.

In large bowl, combine pasta, Veg•All, salmon, soup and pepper.

Pour into greased 3-quart casserole.

Cover; bake 25 minutes or until hot; bake, uncovered, 10 minutes more.   *Makes 6 servings*

Spinach-Potato Bake

SPICY SOUTHERN SUPPERS

Tamale Pie

    1 tablespoon vegetable oil
 ½ cup chopped onion
 ⅓ cup chopped red bell pepper
    1 clove garlic, minced
 ¾ pound ground turkey
 ¾ teaspoon chili powder
 ½ teaspoon dried oregano
    1 can (about 14 ounces) Mexican-style stewed tomatoes
    1 can (about 15 ounces) beans in mild chili sauce, undrained
    1 cup corn
 ¼ teaspoon black pepper
    1 package (8½ ounces) corn muffin mix, plus ingredients to prepare mix
    2 cups (8 ounces) shredded taco cheese blend, divided

1. Heat oil in large skillet over medium heat. Add onion and bell pepper; cook until crisp-tender. Stir in garlic. Add turkey; cook and stir 5 minutes or until no longer pink. Stir in chili powder and oregano. Add tomatoes; cook and stir 2 minutes. Stir in beans, corn and black pepper; simmer 10 minutes or until liquid is reduced by about half.

2. Preheat oven to 375°F. Lightly coat 1½- to 2-quart casserole with nonstick cooking spray. Prepare corn muffin mix according to package directions; stir in ½ cup cheese.

3. Spread half of turkey mixture in prepared casserole; sprinkle with ¾ cup cheese. Top with remaining turkey mixture and ¾ cup cheese. Top with corn muffin batter.

4. Bake 20 to 22 minutes or until light golden brown.   *Makes 4 to 6 servings*

Ham, Poblano and Potato Casserole

¼ cup (½ stick) butter
¼ cup all-purpose flour
1½ cups whole milk
2 pounds baking potatoes, halved and thinly sliced
6 ounces thinly sliced ham, cut into bite-size pieces
1 poblano pepper, cut into thin strips (about 1 cup)
1 cup corn
1 cup chopped red bell pepper
1 cup finely chopped onion
1½ teaspoons salt
¼ teaspoon black pepper
¼ teaspoon ground nutmeg
1½ cups (6 ounces) shredded sharp Cheddar cheese

1. Preheat oven to 350°F. Lightly coat 13×9-inch baking dish with nonstick cooking spray.

2. Melt butter in medium saucepan over medium heat. Add flour; whisk until smooth. Add milk; whisk until smooth. Cook and stir 5 to 7 minutes or until thickened. Remove from heat; set aside.

3. Layer one third of potatoes, half of ham, half of poblano pepper, half of corn, half of bell pepper and half of onion in prepared baking dish. Sprinkle with half of salt, pepper and nutmeg. Repeat layers. Top with remaining third of potatoes. Spoon milk mixture evenly over all.

4. Cover with foil; bake 45 minutes. Uncover; bake 30 minutes or until potatoes are tender. Sprinkle with cheese; bake 5 minutes or until cheese is melted. Let stand 15 minutes before serving.   *Makes 6 servings*

Note: To make this casserole even easier, use a food processor with the slicing blade attachment to thinly slice potatoes.

Ham, Poblano and Potato Casserole

Cajun-Style Beef and Beans

1 pound ground beef
¾ cup chopped onion
2½ cups cooked brown rice
1 can (about 15 ounces) kidney beans, rinsed and drained
1 can (about 14 ounces) stewed tomatoes
2 teaspoons Cajun seasoning
¾ cup (3 ounces) shredded Cheddar cheese

1. Preheat oven to 350°F. Brown beef in large nonstick skillet over medium-high heat 6 to 8 minutes, stirring to break up meat. Drain all but 1 tablespoon fat. Add onion; cook and stir 2 minutes or until translucent. Combine beef mixture, rice, beans, tomatoes and seasoning in 2- to 2½-quart casserole.

2. Cover; bake 25 to 30 minutes, stirring once. Sprinkle with cheese; cover and let stand 5 minutes before serving.

Makes 4 to 6 servings

Tip If you'd like to prepare your own Cajun seasoning, place 5 tablespoons ground red pepper, 3 tablespoons black pepper, 3 tablespoons onion powder, 3 tablespoons garlic powder, 3 tablespoons chili powder, 1 tablespoon dried thyme, 1 tablespoon dried basil and 1 tablespoon ground bay leaf in food processor. Process until the spices are well combined. Stir in ½ cup salt by hand. Store in a tightly sealed container.

Cajun-Style Beef and Beans

Spicy Turkey Casserole

  1 tablespoon olive oil

  1 pound turkey breast cutlets, cut into ½-inch pieces

  2 spicy chicken or turkey sausages (about 3 ounces each), cut into ½-inch-thick slices

  1 cup diced green bell pepper

½ cup sliced mushrooms

½ cup diced onion

  1 jalapeño pepper,* seeded and minced (optional)

½ cup chicken broth

  1 can (about 14 ounces) diced tomatoes

  1 cup hot cooked egg noodles

  1 teaspoon Italian seasoning

½ teaspoon paprika

¼ teaspoon black pepper

  6 tablespoons grated Parmesan cheese

  2 tablespoons coarse plain dry bread crumbs

Jalapeño peppers can sting and irritate the skin, so wear rubber gloves when handling peppers and do not touch your eyes.

1. Preheat oven to 350°F.

2. Heat oil in large nonstick skillet. Add turkey and sausages; cook and stir over medium heat 2 minutes. Add bell pepper, mushrooms, onion and jalapeño pepper, if desired; cook and stir 5 minutes. Add broth; cook 1 minute, stirring to scrape up any browned bits. Stir in tomatoes, noodles, seasoning, paprika and black pepper.

3. Spoon turkey mixture into shallow 10-inch round casserole. Sprinkle with cheese and bread crumbs. Bake 15 to 20 minutes or until heated through and bread crumbs are golden brown.

Makes 4 to 6 servings

E–Z Chicken Tortilla Bake

1 can (10.75 ounces) condensed tomato soup, undiluted
1 cup ORTEGA® Thick & Chunky Salsa
½ cup milk
2 cups cubed cooked chicken
8 (8-inch) ORTEGA® Soft Flour Tortillas, cut into 1-inch pieces
1 cup (4 ounces) shredded Cheddar cheese, divided

Preheat oven to 400°F. Mix soup, salsa, milk, chicken, tortillas and ½ cup cheese in 2-quart shallow baking dish. Cover; bake 30 minutes or until hot. Top with remaining ½ cup cheese.

Makes 4 servings

Note: Two whole chicken breasts (about 10 ounces each) will yield about 2 cups of chopped cooked chicken.

Prep Time: 10 minutes
Start-to-Finish Time: 40 minutes

Picadillo Tamale Casserole

1½ pounds ground beef
1 cup chopped onion
2 cans (about 10 ounces each) diced tomatoes with green chiles
½ cup chicken broth
½ teaspoon ground cinnamon
6 tablespoons slivered almonds
6 tablespoons raisins
2 rolls (1 pound each) prepared polenta, cut into ½-inch-thick slices
2 cups (8 ounces) shredded Mexican cheese blend

1. Preheat oven to 350°F. Brown beef in large nonstick skillet over medium-high heat 6 to 8 minutes, stirring to break up meat. Drain all but 1 tablespoon fat. Add onion; cook and stir 2 minutes or until translucent.

2. Add tomatoes, broth and cinnamon; simmer 2 to 3 minutes. Stir in almonds and raisins.

3. Layer half of polenta slices, half of beef mixture and half of cheese in 13×9-inch casserole. Repeat layers. Bake 25 to 30 minutes or until hot and bubbly. *Makes 8 servings*

E–Z Chicken Tortilla Bake

Shrimp Creole

2 tablespoons olive oil

1½ cups chopped green bell peppers

1 onion, chopped

⅔ cup chopped celery

2 cloves garlic, finely chopped

1 cup uncooked rice

1 can (about 14 ounces) diced tomatoes, drained and juice reserved

2 teaspoons hot pepper sauce

1 teaspoon dried oregano

¾ teaspoon salt

½ teaspoon dried thyme

Black pepper

1 pound medium raw shrimp, peeled

1 tablespoon chopped fresh Italian parsley (optional)

1. Preheat oven to 325°F. Heat oil in large skillet over medium-high heat. Add bell peppers, onion, celery and garlic; cook and stir 5 minutes or until vegetables are tender.

2. Reduce heat to medium. Add rice; cook and stir 5 minutes. Add tomatoes, hot pepper sauce, oregano, salt, thyme and black pepper to skillet; stir until well blended. Pour reserved tomato juice into measuring cup. Add enough water to measure 1¾ cups; add to skillet. Cook and stir 2 minutes.

3. Transfer mixture to 2½-quart casserole. Stir in shrimp. Cover; bake 55 minutes or until rice is tender and liquid is absorbed. Garnish with parsley.   *Makes 4 to 6 servings*

Tip Shrimp are grouped for retail purposes by their size. The count refers to the number of shrimp that make up each pound. The most common sizes are jumbo (11 to 15), large (21 to 30), medium (31 to 35) and small (36 to 45).

Spicy Beefy Noodles

1½ pounds ground beef
1 onion, minced
1 clove garlic, minced
1 tablespoon chili powder
1 teaspoon paprika
⅛ teaspoon dried basil
⅛ teaspoon dried dill weed
⅛ teaspoon dried thyme
⅛ teaspoon dried marjoram
   Salt and black pepper
1 can (about 14 ounces) diced tomatoes with green chiles
1 can (8 ounces) tomato sauce
1 cup water
3 tablespoons Worcestershire sauce
1 package (about 10 ounces) egg noodles
½ cup (2 ounces) *each* shredded Cheddar, mozzarella, pepper jack and provolone cheeses

1. Brown beef in large nonstick skillet over medium-high heat 6 to 8 minutes, stirring to break up meat. Drain all but 1 tablespoon fat. Add onion; cook and stir 2 minutes or until translucent. Add garlic; cook and stir 30 seconds. Stir in chili powder, paprika, basil, dill, thyme and marjoram; cook and stir 2 minutes. Season with salt and pepper.

2. Add tomatoes, tomato sauce, water and Worcestershire sauce; mix well. Cover; simmer 20 minutes. Meanwhile, cook noodles according to package directions. Keep warm.

3. Combine beef mixture and noodles in 2-quart microwavable casserole. Combine cheeses in medium bowl; sprinkle evenly over top.

4. Microwave on HIGH 3 minutes. Let stand 5 minutes. Microwave 3 minutes or until cheeses are melted.   *Makes 6 servings*

Gumbo Casserole

2 cans (10¾ ounces each) CAMPBELL'S® Condensed Chicken Gumbo Soup
1 soup can water
1 teaspoon dried minced onion
½ teaspoon Cajun seasoning
½ teaspoon garlic powder
1 cup frozen okra, thawed
¾ cup uncooked instant white rice
½ pound cooked ham, diced (about 1½ cups)
½ pound cooked shrimp, peeled and deveined

1. Heat the oven to 375°F. Stir the soup, water, onion, Cajun seasoning, garlic powder, okra, rice, ham and shrimp in a 2-quart casserole.

2. Bake for 35 minutes or until the gumbo is hot and bubbling. Stir the gumbo before serving.

Makes 4 servings

Kitchen Tip: Try stirring in a little diced andouille sausage for even more Cajun-style flavor!

Prep Time: 15 minutes
Bake Time: 35 minutes

Enticing Enchiladas

1 tablespoon vegetable oil
1 green or red bell pepper, chopped
½ cup chopped onion
4 cloves garlic, minced
1 package JENNIE-O TURKEY STORE® Lean Ground Turkey
1 tablespoon Mexican seasoning or chili powder
2 cans (10 ounces each) mild enchilada sauce, divided
2 cups (8 ounces) shredded Mexican cheese blend or Monterey Jack cheese, divided
12 (7-inch) soft flour tortillas or flavored flour tortillas
1 cup shredded lettuce
½ cup diced tomato
   Ripe avocado slices (optional)

continued on page 40

Gumbo Casserole

Enticing Enchiladas, continued

Heat oven to 375°F. Heat oil in large skillet over medium heat. Add bell pepper, onion and garlic; cook 5 minutes, stirring occasionally. Crumble turkey into skillet; sprinkle with seasoning. Cook about 8 minutes or until no longer pink, stirring occasionally. Stir in ½ cup enchilada sauce. Remove from heat; stir in 1 cup cheese. Spread ½ cup enchilada sauce over bottom of 13×9-inch baking dish. Spoon about ⅓ cup turkey mixture down center of each tortilla. Fold bottom of tortilla up over filling, fold in sides and roll up. Place, seam side down, in prepared dish. Spoon remaining enchilada sauce evenly over enchiladas. Cover with foil; bake 20 minutes. Sprinkle with remaining 1 cup cheese. Return to oven; bake, uncovered, 10 minutes or until cheese is melted and sauce is bubbly. Garnish with lettuce and tomato. Top with avocado, if desired. *Makes 6 servings*

Prep Time: 30 minutes
Cook Time: 45 minutes

Beefy Texas Cheddar Bake

1½ **pounds ground beef**
1 **cup chopped onion**
2 **cans (10¾ ounces each) condensed tomato soup, preferably Mexican-style, undiluted**
2 **cups beef broth**
1 **box (6 ounces) corn bread stuffing mix**
¼ **cup (½ stick) butter, melted**
2 **teaspoons ground cumin**
2 **teaspoons ground chili powder**
2 **cups (8 ounces) shredded Mexican cheese blend**

1. Preheat oven to 350°F. Lightly coat 3-quart casserole with nonstick cooking spray.

2. Brown beef in large nonstick skillet over medium-high heat 6 to 8 minutes, stirring to break up meat. Drain all but 1 tablespoon fat. Add onion; cook and stir 2 minutes or until translucent. Transfer to prepared casserole.

3. Mix soups, broth, stuffing mix, butter, cumin and chili powder in large bowl until combined. Spoon evenly over beef mixture. Top with cheese.

4. Bake 30 minutes or until heated through. *Makes 8 servings*

Beefy Texas Cheddar Bake

Kids' Choice Casseroles

Cheddar Tuna Noodles

2 tablespoons butter

½ cup chopped onion

½ cup chopped celery

2 tablespoons all-purpose flour

½ teaspoon salt

¼ teaspoon red pepper flakes (optional)

2 cups milk

8 ounces uncooked egg noodles, cooked and drained

2 cans (6 ounces each) white tuna packed in water, drained and flaked

1 cup frozen peas

½ cup (2 ounces) shredded Cheddar cheese

1. Preheat oven to 375°F. Lightly coat 9-inch square baking dish with nonstick cooking spray.

2. Melt butter in large skillet over medium heat. Add onion; cook and stir 3 minutes. Add celery; cook and stir 3 minutes.

3. Sprinkle flour, salt and red pepper flakes, if desired, over onion mixture; cook and stir 2 minutes. Gradually whisk in milk; bring to a boil. Cook and stir 2 minutes or until thickened. Remove from heat.

4. Combine noodles, milk mixture, tuna and peas in prepared baking dish; toss to coat. Sprinkle with cheese. Bake 20 to 25 minutes or until hot and bubbly.   *Makes 4 to 6 servings*

Sausage Pizza Pie Casserole

8 ounces mild Italian sausage, casings removed
1 package (about 14 ounces) refrigerated pizza dough
½ cup tomato sauce
2 tablespoons chopped fresh basil *or* 2 teaspoons dried basil
½ teaspoon dried oregano
¼ teaspoon red pepper flakes (optional)
3 ounces mushrooms, quartered
½ cup thinly sliced red onion
½ cup thinly sliced green bell pepper
½ cup seeded diced tomato
½ cup sliced pitted black olives
8 slices smoked provolone cheese
2 tablespoons grated Parmesan and Romano cheese blend

1. Preheat oven to 350°F. Lightly coat 13×9-inch baking dish with nonstick cooking spray.

2. Brown sausage in large nonstick skillet over medium-high heat 6 to 8 minutes, stirring to break up meat. Drain fat.

3. Line prepared baking dish with pizza dough. Spoon sauce evenly over dough; sprinkle with basil, oregano and red pepper flakes, if desired. Layer with sausage, mushrooms, onion, bell pepper, tomato, olives and provolone cheese. Roll down sides of crust to form rim.

4. Bake 20 to 25 minutes or until bottom and sides of crust are golden brown. Sprinkle with cheese blend; let stand 5 minutes before serving.   *Makes 4 to 6 servings*

Sausage Pizza Pie Casserole

Chicken Pot Pie

1½ pounds bone-in chicken thighs or breasts, skinned
1 cup chicken broth
½ teaspoon salt
¼ teaspoon black pepper
1 to 1½ cups milk
3 tablespoons butter
1 onion, chopped
1 cup sliced celery
⅓ cup all-purpose flour
2 cups frozen mixed vegetables (broccoli, carrots and cauliflower), thawed
1 tablespoon chopped fresh Italian parsley *or* 1 teaspoon dried parsley flakes
½ teaspoon dried thyme
1 (9-inch) refrigerated pie crust
1 egg, lightly beaten

1. Combine chicken, broth, salt and pepper in large saucepan over medium-high heat; bring to a boil. Reduce heat to low. Cover; simmer 30 minutes or until chicken is cooked through (165°F).

2. Remove chicken and let cool. Pour remaining chicken broth mixture into glass measure. Let stand; spoon off fat. Add enough milk to broth mixture to equal 2½ cups. Remove chicken from bones and cut into ½-inch pieces.

3. Preheat oven to 400°F. Melt butter in same saucepan over medium heat. Add onion and celery; cook and stir 3 minutes or until tender. Stir in flour until well blended. Gradually stir in broth mixture. Cook, stirring constantly, until sauce thickens and boils. Add chicken, vegetables, parsley and thyme. Pour into 1½-quart casserole.

4. Roll out pie crust to 1 inch larger than diameter of casserole on lightly floured surface. Cut slits in crust to vent; place on top of casserole. Roll edges and cut away extra dough; flute edges. If desired, reroll scraps to cut into decorative designs; place on crust. Brush with beaten egg. Bake 30 minutes until crust is golden brown and filling is bubbly.   *Makes 4 servings*

Note: You can substitute 2 cups diced cooked chicken for chicken thighs. Increase chicken broth to 1 (14-ounce) can. Decrease salt to ¼ teaspoon. Combine broth, salt and pepper in glass measure. Add milk to equal 2½ cups. Process as directed in step 3.

Chicken Pot Pie

Chili Wagon Wheel Casserole

8 ounces uncooked wagon wheel or other pasta
Nonstick cooking spray
1 pound ground turkey
¾ cup *each* chopped onion and green bell pepper
1 can (about 14 ounces) stewed tomatoes
1 can (8 ounces) tomato sauce
¼ teaspoon ground allspice
Salt and black pepper
½ cup (2 ounces) shredded Cheddar cheese

1. Preheat oven to 350°F. Cook pasta according to package directions. Drain well; cover and keep warm.

2. Lightly coat large nonstick skillet with cooking spray. Add turkey; cook and stir over medium-high heat 5 minutes or until no longer pink. Add onion and bell pepper; cook and stir until tender.

3. Stir in tomatoes, tomato sauce and allspice; cook 2 minutes. Season with salt and black pepper. Stir in pasta. Spoon mixture into 2½-quart casserole. Sprinkle with cheese. Bake 20 to 25 minutes or until heated through. *Makes 4 to 6 servings*

Lit'l Smokies Macaroni and Cheese

1 package (16 ounces) HILLSHIRE FARM® Lit'l Smokies®
1 package (7¼ ounces) macaroni and cheese mix
⅓ cup milk
¼ cup butter or margarine
1 can (10¾ ounces) condensed cream of mushroom or cream of celery soup
1 tablespoon finely chopped parsley
1 cup (4 ounces) shredded Cheddar cheese

1. Preheat oven to 350°F. Open package of Lit'l Smokies® and drain off any liquid; set aside. Cook macaroni in a large pan of boiling water for 7 minutes or until tender; drain well.

2. In medium bowl combine cooked macaroni, contents of cheese sauce packet, milk and butter. Stir until butter is melted. Stir in mushroom soup, parsley and Lit'l Smokies®.

3. Place mixture in a greased 2-quart baking dish. Sprinkle with Cheddar cheese. Bake, uncovered, 20 minutes or until heated through. *Makes 6 servings*

Chili Wagon Wheel Casserole

Family-Style Frankfurters with Rice and Red Beans

  1 tablespoon vegetable oil
  1 onion, chopped
½ green bell pepper, chopped
  2 cloves garlic, minced
  1 can (about 15 ounces) red kidney beans, rinsed and drained
  1 can (about 15 ounces) Great Northern beans, rinsed and drained
½ pound beef frankfurters, cut into ¼-inch-thick pieces
  1 cup uncooked instant brown rice
  1 cup vegetable broth
¼ cup packed brown sugar
¼ cup ketchup
  3 tablespoons dark molasses
  1 tablespoon Dijon mustard

1. Preheat oven to 350°F. Lightly coat 13×9-inch baking dish with nonstick cooking spray.

2. Heat oil in Dutch oven over medium-high heat. Add onion, bell pepper and garlic; cook and stir 2 minutes or until tender.

3. Add beans, frankfurters, rice, broth, brown sugar, ketchup, molasses and mustard to vegetables; stir to blend. Transfer to prepared baking dish.

4. Cover tightly with foil; bake 30 minutes or until rice is tender.   *Makes 6 servings*

Tip Great Northern beans are large white beans that have a delicate flavor. They can be used in casseroles, soups, stews, baked beans and salads. Great Northern beans are available both dried and canned.

Cheesy Chicken Bake

    1 can (10¾ ounces) CAMPBELL'S® Condensed Cream of Chicken Soup (Regular or 98% Fat Free)
  1⅓ cups water
    1 teaspoon Worcestershire sauce
    ¾ cup uncooked regular long-grain white rice
    2 cups cubed cooked chicken
    ½ cup shredded Cheddar cheese
    1 can (2.8 ounces) French fried onions (1⅓ cups)

1. Stir the soup, water, Worcestershire, rice, chicken and cheese in a 2-quart casserole. **Cover.**

2. Bake at 350°F. for 35 minutes or until hot. Stir.

3. Sprinkle with onions. Bake for 5 minutes more or until golden.
        Makes 4 servings

Prep Time: 5 minutes
Bake Time: 40 minutes

Rainbow Casserole

    5 potatoes, peeled and cut into thin slices
    1 pound ground beef
    1 onion, halved and thinly sliced
      Salt and black pepper
    1 can (about 28 ounces) stewed tomatoes, drained and juice reserved
    1 cup frozen peas *or* 1 can (about 6 ounces) peas, drained

1. Preheat oven to 350°F. Lightly coat 3-quart casserole with nonstick cooking spray.

2. Combine potatoes and enough salted water to cover in large saucepan. Bring to a boil. Reduce heat; simmer 15 minutes or until almost tender. Drain.

3. Meanwhile, brown beef 6 to 8 minutes in large skillet over medium-high heat, stirring to break up meat. Drain fat.

4. Layer half of beef, half of potatoes, half of onion, salt, pepper, half of tomatoes and half of peas. Repeat layers. Add reserved tomato juice.

5. Cover; bake 40 minutes or until most of liquid is absorbed.
        Makes 4 servings

Cheesy Chicken Bake

Split-Biscuit Chicken Pie

⅓ **cup butter**
⅓ **cup all-purpose flour**
2½ **cups whole milk**
1 **tablespoon chicken bouillon granules**
½ **teaspoon dried thyme**
½ **teaspoon black pepper**
4 **cups diced cooked chicken**
2 **jars (4 ounces each) diced pimientos**
1 **cup frozen peas, thawed**
1 **package (6 ounces) refrigerated biscuit dough**

1. Preheat oven to 350°F. Lightly coat 12×8-inch baking dish or 2-quart casserole with nonstick cooking spray.

2. Melt butter in large skillet over medium heat. Add flour; mix until smooth. Add milk, bouillon, thyme and pepper; mix until smooth. Cook and stir until thickened. Remove from heat. Stir in chicken, pimientos and peas. Pour mixture into prepared baking dish. Bake 30 minutes.

3. Meanwhile, bake biscuits according to package directions.

4. Split biscuits in half; arrange cut side down on top of chicken mixture. Bake 3 minutes or until biscuits are heated through.   *Makes 4 to 5 servings*

Tip Grown mostly in Spain, the pimiento is most famous for stuffing green olives. (Pimiento means "pepper" in Spanish.) However, most of the crop is ground into paprika. Pimientos are available in jars in most large supermarkets.

No-Fuss Lasagna

1 package (approximately 1 pound) JOHNSONVILLE® Italian Sausage Links
1 jar (26 ounces) pasta sauce
1 cup water
1 carton (15 ounces) ricotta or cottage cheese
1 egg
1 tablespoon dried parsley flakes
½ teaspoon dried oregano
8 lasagna noodles, uncooked
4 cups (16 ounces) shredded mozzarella cheese
    Parmesan cheese, optional
    Sliced black olives, optional

Pan-fry or broil sausage according to package directions. Cut sausage in half lengthwise, then into ¼-inch slices. In a large skillet, combine the sausage, pasta sauce and water. Bring to a boil; reduce heat and simmer, uncovered, for 5 minutes.

In a bowl, combine the ricotta cheese, egg, parsley and oregano. Spread one third of the pasta sauce mixture over the bottom of a greased 13×9-inch baking dish. Layer with half of the noodles and half of the ricotta cheese mixture. Sprinkle with half of the mozzarella cheese. Top with a third of the sauce. Layer with the remaining noodles, ricotta cheese mixture and mozzarella cheese. Top with the remaining sauce. Sprinkle with Parmesan cheese and black olives, if desired. Cover and refrigerate for at least 8 hours or overnight.

Remove lasagna from the refrigerator 30 minutes before baking. Bake, uncovered, at 350°F for about 1 hour or until noodles are tender and sauce is bubbly. Let stand 5 to 10 minutes before serving.   *Makes 10 servings*

Sloppy Joe Casserole

  1 pound ground beef
  1 can (10¾ ounces) CAMPBELL'S® Condensed Tomato Soup (Regular or Healthy Request®)
¼ cup water
  1 teaspoon Worcestershire sauce
⅛ teaspoon ground black pepper
  1 package (7.5 ounces) refrigerated biscuits (10 biscuits)
½ cup shredded Cheddar cheese

1. Heat the oven to 400°F.

2. Cook the beef in a 10-inch skillet over medium-high heat until it's well browned, stirring often to separate meat. Pour off any fat.

3. Stir the soup, water, Worcestershire and black pepper in the skillet and heat to a boil. Spoon the beef mixture into a 1½-quart casserole. Arrange the biscuits around the inside edge of the casserole.

4. Bake for 15 minutes or until the biscuits are golden brown. Sprinkle the cheese over the beef mixture.

Makes 5 servings

Ham & Cheese Grits Puff

  3 cups water
¾ cup quick-cooking grits
½ teaspoon salt
½ cup (2 ounces) shredded mozzarella cheese
  2 ounces ham, finely chopped
  2 tablespoons minced fresh chives (optional)
  2 eggs, separated

1. Preheat oven to 375°F. Grease 1½-quart soufflé dish or deep casserole.

2. Bring water to a boil in medium saucepan. Stir in grits and salt. Cook and stir 5 minutes or until thickened. Stir in cheese, ham, chives, if desired, and egg yolks.

3. Beat egg whites in small bowl until stiff but not dry; fold into grits mixture. Spoon into prepared dish. Bake 30 minutes or until puffed and golden. Serve immediately.

Makes 4 to 6 servings

Sloppy Joe Casserole

INTERNATIONAL FLAVORS

Greek Chicken & Spinach Rice Casserole

Nonstick cooking spray
1 cup finely chopped onion
1 package (10 ounces) frozen chopped spinach, thawed and squeezed dry
1 cup uncooked quick-cooking brown rice
1 cup water
¼ teaspoon salt
⅛ teaspoon ground red pepper
1 pound chicken tenders
2 teaspoons dried Greek seasoning (oregano, rosemary and sage mixture)
½ teaspoon lemon-pepper seasoning
1 tablespoon olive oil
1 lemon, cut into wedges

1. Preheat oven to 350°F. Lightly coat large ovenproof skillet with cooking spray; heat over medium heat. Add onion; cook and stir 2 minutes or until translucent. Add spinach, rice, water, salt and red pepper. Stir until well blended. Remove from heat.

2. Place chicken on top of mixture in skillet in single layer. Sprinkle with Greek seasoning and lemon-pepper seasoning. Cover with foil.

3. Bake 25 minutes or until chicken is no longer pink in center.

4. Remove foil. Drizzle oil evenly over top. Serve with lemon wedges.   *Makes 4 servings*

Midweek Moussaka

1 eggplant (about 1 pound), cut into ¼-inch slices
2 tablespoons olive oil
1 pound ground beef
1 can (about 14 ounces) stewed tomatoes, drained
¼ cup red wine
2 tablespoons tomato paste
2 teaspoons sugar
¾ teaspoon salt
½ teaspoon dried oregano
¼ teaspoon ground cinnamon
¼ teaspoon black pepper
⅛ teaspoon ground allspice
½ (8-ounce) package cream cheese
¼ cup milk
¼ cup grated Parmesan cheese
Additional ground cinnamon (optional)

1. Preheat broiler. Lightly coat 8-inch square baking dish with nonstick cooking spray.

2. Line baking sheet with foil. Arrange eggplant slices on foil, overlapping slightly if necessary. Brush with oil; broil 5 to 6 inches from heat 4 minutes on each side. *Reduce oven temperature to 350°F.*

3. Meanwhile, brown beef in large nonstick skillet over medium-high heat 6 to 8 minutes, stirring to break up meat. Drain fat. Add tomatoes, wine, tomato paste, sugar, salt, oregano, cinnamon, pepper and allspice. Bring to a boil, breaking up large pieces of tomato with spoon. Reduce heat to medium-low; cover and simmer 10 minutes,

4. Place cream cheese and milk in small microwavable bowl. Cover and microwave on HIGH 1 minute.* Stir with fork until smooth.

5. Arrange half of eggplant slices in prepared baking dish. Spoon half of meat sauce over eggplant; sprinkle with half of Parmesan cheese. Repeat layers. Spoon cream cheese mixture evenly over top. Bake 20 minutes or until top begins to crack slightly. Sprinkle lightly with additional cinnamon, if desired. Let stand 10 minutes before serving.   *Makes 4 servings*

Or place in small saucepan over medium heat and stir until cream cheese is melted.

Cheesy Mexican Casserole

  1 cup uncooked rice
¾ pound ground beef
¾ cup mild picante sauce
  1 teaspoon ground cumin
  2 cups (8 ounces) shredded sharp Cheddar cheese, divided
½ cup sour cream
⅓ cup finely chopped green onions
  2 tablespoons chopped fresh cilantro
½ teaspoon salt
⅛ teaspoon ground red pepper

1. Cook rice according to package directions.

2. Preheat oven to 350°F. Lightly coat 11×7-inch baking dish with nonstick cooking spray.

3. Brown beef in large nonstick skillet over medium-high heat 6 to 8 minutes, stirring to break up meat. Drain fat. Add picante sauce and cumin; stir well.

4. Stir 1 cup cheese, sour cream, green onions, cilantro, salt and red pepper into rice. Spoon rice mixture into prepared baking dish. Top with beef mixture.

5. Cover with foil; bake 20 minutes or until heated through. Sprinkle with remaining 1 cup cheese. Bake, uncovered, 3 minutes or until cheese melts.   *Makes 4 servings*

Tip Cumin is used extensively in Mexican, Middle Eastern, North African and Indian cooking. It is a primary ingredient of garam masala, the traditional spice mixture from Northern India, and is often found in chili powders as well. Cumin is a delicious addition to stews, casseroles, marinades and barbecue sauces.

Spinach and Mushroom Enchiladas

2 packages (10 ounces each) frozen chopped spinach, thawed and squeezed dry
1½ cups sliced mushrooms
1 can (about 15 ounces) pinto beans, rinsed and drained
3 teaspoons chili powder, divided
¼ teaspoon red pepper flakes
1 can (8 ounces) tomato sauce
2 tablespoons water
½ teaspoon hot pepper sauce
8 (8-inch) corn tortillas
1 cup (4 ounces) shredded Monterey Jack cheese
Shredded lettuce (optional)
Chopped tomatoes (optional)
Sour cream (optional)
Chopped fresh cilantro (optional)

1. Cook and stir spinach, mushrooms, beans, 2 teaspoons chili powder and red pepper flakes in large skillet over medium heat 5 minutes.

2. Combine tomato sauce, water, remaining 1 teaspoon chili powder and hot pepper sauce in medium skillet. Dip tortillas into tomato sauce mixture; stack tortillas on waxed paper.

3. Divide spinach filling into 8 portions. Spoon onto center of tortillas; roll up and place, seam side down, in 11×8-inch microwavable dish. Secure rolls with toothpicks, if necessary. Spread remaining tomato sauce mixture over enchiladas.

4. Cover with vented plastic wrap. Microwave on MEDIUM (50%) 10 minutes or until heated through. Sprinkle with cheese. Microwave on MEDIUM (50%) 3 minutes or until cheese is melted. Serve with lettuce, tomatoes, sour cream and cilantro, if desired. Remove and discard toothpicks before serving. *Makes 4 servings*

Spinach and Mushroom Enchiladas

Creamy Beef, Carrot and Noodle Baked Stroganoff

1 pound ground beef
1 large onion, diced (about 1 cup)
2 cans (10¾ ounces each) CAMPBELL'S® Condensed Cream of Mushroom Soup (Regular or 98% Fat Free)
2 cups water
2 cups frozen crinkle-cut carrots, thawed
2 cups uncooked medium egg noodles
½ cup sour cream

1. Cook the beef and onion in a 12-inch skillet until the beef is well browned, stirring frequently to separate meat. Pour off any fat. Spoon the beef mixture into a 13×9×2-inch (3-quart) shallow baking dish. Stir the soup, water, carrots, noodles and sour cream into the dish. **Cover.**

2. Bake at 375°F. for 30 minutes or until hot and bubbly.   *Makes 6 servings*

Oven Pork Cassoulet

1 tablespoon canola oil
1¼ pounds pork tenderloin, cut into 1-inch pieces
1 cup chopped onion
1 cup chopped carrots
3 cloves garlic, minced
2 cans (about 15 ounces each) cannellini beans, rinsed and drained
1 can (about 14 ounces) diced tomatoes with Italian seasoning
¼ pound smoked turkey sausage, cut into ¼-inch-thick slices
1 teaspoon dried thyme
¼ teaspoon *each* salt, dried rosemary and black pepper

1. Preheat oven to 325°F. Heat oil in Dutch oven over medium heat; brown pork in batches. Transfer pork to plate.

2. Add onion, carrots and garlic to Dutch oven; cook and stir 8 to 10 minutes or until tender.

3. Combine pork, onion mixture, beans, tomatoes, sausage, thyme, salt, rosemary and pepper in 3-quart casserole. Cover; bake 35 to 40 minutes or until pork is barely pink in center.

Makes 6 servings

Creamy Beef, Carrot and Noodle Baked Stroganoff

Athens Casserole

2 tablespoons vegetable oil
1½ pounds eggplant, peeled and cut crosswise into ¼-inch slices
1½ pounds ground beef
2 cups chopped onions
1 green bell pepper, cut into strips
1 yellow bell pepper, cut into strips
1 red bell pepper, cut into strips
¼ cup chopped fresh Italian parsley
¼ cup dry red wine
1 teaspoon garlic powder
1 teaspoon ground cinnamon
Salt and black pepper
2 cans (28 ounces each) stewed tomatoes
8 ounces feta cheese, crumbled
4 eggs, beaten
½ cup plain dry bread crumbs

1. Preheat oven to 350°F.

2. Heat oil in large skillet over medium-high heat. Add eggplant and brown on both sides, 5 to 7 minutes; set aside on paper towels to drain.

3. Add beef to same skillet; brown 6 to 8 minutes, stirring to break up meat. Drain all but 1 tablespoon fat. Add onions and bell peppers; cook and stir until tender. Add parsley, wine, garlic powder and cinnamon; mix well. Season with salt and black pepper.

4. Pour one third of tomatoes into 13×9-inch baking dish. Layer with one third of eggplant, one third of beef mixture and one third of cheese. Repeat layers twice. Pour eggs over top and sprinkle with bread crumbs.

5. Bake 45 minutes or until heated through and bubbly.   *Makes 10 servings*

Caribbean Black Bean Casserole with Spicy Mango Salsa

2 cups chicken broth
1 cup uncooked basmati rice
2 tablespoons olive oil, divided
½ pound Spanish-style chorizo sausage links
1 cup chopped red bell pepper
2 cloves garlic, minced
3 cups canned black beans, rinsed and drained
½ cup chopped fresh cilantro
2 small mangoes
1 cup chopped red onion
2 tablespoons honey
2 tablespoons white wine vinegar
1 teaspoon curry powder
½ teaspoon salt
½ teaspoon ground red pepper

1. Bring broth to a boil in medium saucepan over high heat; stir in rice. Reduce heat to low. Cover; simmer 20 minutes or until liquid is absorbed and rice is tender.

2. Preheat oven to 350°F. Lightly coat 1½-quart casserole with nonstick cooking spray.

3. Heat 1 tablespoon oil in large skillet over medium heat. Add sausage; cook, turning occasionally, 8 to 10 minutes until browned and cooked through. Drain fat. Cut into ½-inch slices; set aside.

4. Add remaining 1 tablespoon oil to same skillet; heat over medium-high heat. Add bell pepper; cook and stir until tender. Add garlic; cook and stir 30 seconds. Remove from heat. Stir in beans, sausage, rice and cilantro. Spoon mixture into prepared casserole.

5. Cover with foil; bake 30 minutes or until heated through.

6. Meanwhile, peel mangoes; remove and discard pits. Chop enough flesh to measure 3 cups. Combine mango, onion, honey, vinegar, curry power, salt and red pepper in large bowl. Serve with casserole.   *Makes 6 servings*

Pastitsio

8 ounces uncooked ziti pasta or elbow macaroni
1 pound ground lamb or beef
½ cup chopped onion
1 clove garlic, finely chopped
1 can (8 ounces) tomato sauce
½ teaspoon dried oregano
½ teaspoon black pepper
¼ teaspoon ground cinnamon
2 tablespoons butter
2 tablespoons all-purpose flour
1½ cups milk
1 egg
1 cup grated Parmesan cheese, divided

1. Preheat oven to 350°F. Lightly coat 9-inch baking dish with nonstick cooking spray.

2. Cook pasta according to package directions. Drain well; cover and keep warm.

3. Brown lamb in large nonstick skillet over medium-high heat 6 to 8 minutes, stirring to break up meat. Drain all but 1 tablespoon fat. Add onion; cook and stir 2 minutes or until translucent. Add garlic; cook and stir 30 seconds. Stir in tomato sauce, oregano, pepper and cinnamon. Reduce heat to low; simmer 10 minutes.

4. Spread half of pasta in prepared dish. Top with lamb mixture, then remaining pasta.

5. For sauce, melt butter in medium saucepan over medium-low heat. Whisk in flour. Cook 1 minute, whisking constantly. Whisk in milk. Cook 6 minutes or until thickened, whisking frequently. Beat egg in small bowl; stir in some of sauce. Return egg mixture to saucepan; cook 2 minutes, whisking frequently. Remove from heat; stir in ¾ cup Parmesan cheese until smooth.

6. Pour sauce over top. Sprinkle with remaining ¼ cup Parmesan cheese. Bake 30 minutes or until heated through and golden brown. *Makes 6 servings*

Cacciatore Noodle Casserole

    2 cups PREGO® Traditional Italian Sauce
¾ cup water
    1 cup frozen Italian-style vegetable combination
    1 jar (4.5 ounces) sliced mushrooms, drained
    3 cups cubed cooked chicken
    3 cups medium egg noodles, cooked and drained
¼ cup grated Parmesan cheese

1. Stir the sauce, water, Italian vegetables, mushrooms, chicken and noodles in a 2-quart casserole.

2. Bake at 400°F. for 25 minutes or until hot. Stir.

3. Sprinkle with the cheese. *Makes 6 servings*

Easy Substitution Tip: Use leftover cubed rotisserie chicken or drained canned chicken for the cubed cooked chicken.

Chicken Vera Cruz

    1 chicken (3 pounds), cut up
    1 jar (12 ounces) salsa
1⅓ cups *French's*® French Fried Onions, divided
½ cup Spanish stuffed olives, sliced
½ cup beer or nonalcoholic malt beverage
    2 tablespoons lemon juice
    2 tablespoons chopped fresh parsley *or* 1 tablespoon dried parsley flakes
¼ teaspoon ground black pepper
    Cooked white rice (optional)

1. Preheat oven to 350°F. Place chicken in 2-quart shallow dish. Bake, uncovered, 40 minutes. Drain.

2. Combine salsa, ⅔ *cup* French Fried Onions, olives, beer, lemon juice, parsley and pepper in medium saucepan. Bring to a boil. Reduce heat to low. Cook and stir 5 minutes or until slightly thickened. Pour sauce over chicken. Bake 15 minutes or until chicken is no longer pink near bone. Sprinkle with remaining ⅔ *cup* onions. Bake 5 minutes or until onions are golden. Serve with rice, if desired. *Makes 4 to 6 servings*

Cacciatore Noodle Casserole

Mediterranean-Style Tuna Noodle Casserole

   1 tablespoon extra-virgin olive oil
   4 cloves garlic, minced
   2 large onions, chopped (1½ cups)
 12 ounces mushrooms, chopped (4 cups)
   2 large tomatoes, chopped
   1 red bell pepper, diced (1 cup)
   1 green bell pepper, diced (1 cup)
   1 cup chopped fresh cilantro leaves *or* ¼ cup dried oregano leaves
   2 tablespoons dried marjoram or oregano leaves
   1 to 2 teaspoons ground red pepper
   1 pound JARLSBERG LITE™ cheese, shredded (4 cups)
   1 (16-ounce) can black-eyed peas, rinsed and drained
   2 (7-ounce) cans tuna, drained and flaked
   6 ounces cooked pasta (tricolor rotelle, bows or macaroni)

Preheat oven to 350°F. Heat oil in large skillet; sauté garlic until golden. Add onions; sauté until transparent, about 2 minutes on medium-high heat.

Add mushrooms, tomatoes and bell peppers; cook and stir 3 to 5 minutes or until mushrooms begin to brown. Add cilantro, marjoram and ground red pepper.

Toss with cheese, peas, tuna and pasta. Pour into greased baking dish. Bake, covered, 45 minutes or until cooked through. *Makes 6 to 8 servings*

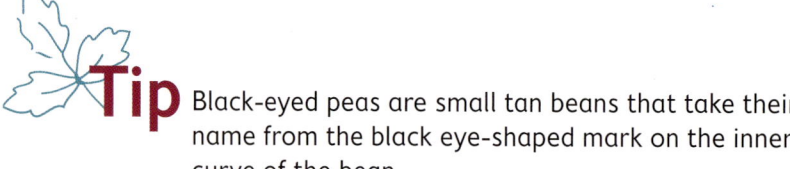

Tip Black-eyed peas are small tan beans that take their name from the black eye-shaped mark on the inner curve of the bean.

Apple Curry Chicken

　　4 boneless skinless chicken breasts
　　1 cup apple juice, divided
　1/4 teaspoon salt
　　　Dash black pepper
1 1/2 cups plain croutons
　　1 apple, chopped
　　1 onion, chopped
　1/4 cup raisins
　　2 teaspoons brown sugar
　　1 teaspoon curry powder
　3/4 teaspoon poultry seasoning
　1/8 teaspoon garlic powder

1. Preheat oven to 350°F. Lightly coat 2-quart baking dish with nonstick cooking spray.

2. Arrange chicken in single layer in prepared baking dish. Combine 1/4 cup apple juice, salt and pepper in small bowl. Brush juice mixture over chicken.

3. Combine croutons, apple, onion, raisins, brown sugar, curry powder, seasoning and garlic powder in large bowl. Toss with remaining 3/4 cup apple juice.

4. Spoon crouton mixture over chicken. Cover with foil; bake 45 minutes or until chicken is no longer pink in center.　　　　　　　　　　　　　　*Makes 4 servings*

Easy Chicken Chalupas

　　1 rotisserie chicken (about 2 pounds)
　　8 (8-inch) flour tortillas
　　2 cups (8 ounces) shredded Cheddar cheese
　　1 cup mild green salsa
　　1 cup mild red salsa

1. Preheat oven to 350°F. Lightly coat 13×9-inch baking dish with nonstick cooking spray.

2. Shred chicken; discard skin and bones.

3. Place 2 tortillas in bottom of prepared dish, overlapping slightly. Layer tortillas with 1 cup chicken, 1/2 cup cheese and 1/4 cup of each salsa. Repeat layers three times.

4. Bake 25 minutes or until bubbly and heated through.　　　　　　*Makes 4 servings*

Apple Curry Chicken

Sweet & Sour Chicken and Rice

1 pound chicken tenders

1 can (8 ounces) pineapple chunks, drained and juice reserved

1 cup uncooked rice

2 carrots, thinly sliced

1 green bell pepper, cut into 1-inch pieces

1 onion, chopped

3 cloves garlic, minced

1 can (about 14 ounces) chicken broth

⅓ cup soy sauce

3 tablespoons sugar

3 tablespoons apple cider vinegar

1 tablespoon sesame oil

1½ teaspoons ground ginger

¼ cup chopped peanuts (optional)

Chopped fresh cilantro (optional)

1. Preheat oven to 350°F. Lightly coat 13×9-inch baking dish with nonstick cooking spray.

2. Combine chicken, pineapple, rice, carrots, bell pepper, onion and garlic in prepared baking dish.

3. Place broth, reserved pineapple juice, soy sauce, sugar, vinegar, sesame oil and ginger in small saucepan; bring to a boil over high heat. Pour over chicken mixture.

4. Cover with foil. Bake 40 to 50 minutes or until chicken is no longer pink in center and rice is tender. Sprinkle with peanuts and cilantro, if desired. *Makes 6 servings*

TABLE OF CONTENTS

HEARTY BOWLS

Turkey Vegetable Chili Mac

Nonstick cooking spray
¾ pound ground turkey
1 can (about 15 ounces) black beans, rinsed and drained
1 can (about 14 ounces) Mexican-style diced tomatoes
1 can (about 14 ounces) diced tomatoes
1 cup frozen corn
½ cup chopped onion
2 cloves garlic, minced
1 teaspoon Mexican seasoning
1 cup uncooked elbow macaroni
⅓ cup sour cream

Slow Cooker Directions

1. Lightly coat large nonstick skillet with nonstick cooking spray. Add turkey; cook and stir 5 minutes or until no longer pink. Transfer to slow cooker.

2. Add beans, tomatoes, corn, onion, garlic and seasoning. Cover; cook on LOW 4 to 5 hours.

3. Stir in macaroni. Cover; cook 10 minutes. Stir. Cover; cook 20 to 30 minutes or until macaroni is tender. Serve with sour cream.

Makes 4 to 6 servings

Chinese Chicken Stew

    1 pound boneless skinless chicken thighs, cut into 1-inch pieces
    1 teaspoon Chinese five-spice powder*
    ½ to ¾ teaspoon red pepper flakes
    1 tablespoon peanut or vegetable oil
    1 onion, coarsely chopped
    1 package (8 ounces) mushrooms, sliced
    2 cloves garlic, minced
    1 can (about 14 ounces) chicken broth, divided
    1 tablespoon cornstarch
    1 red bell pepper, cut into ¾-inch pieces
    2 tablespoons soy sauce
    2 green onions, cut into ½-inch pieces
    1 tablespoon dark sesame oil
    3 cups hot cooked white rice
    ¼ cup coarsely chopped fresh cilantro (optional)

Chinese five-spice powder is a blend of cinnamon, cloves, fennel seed, anise and Szechuan peppercorns. It is available in most supermarkets and at Asian grocery stores.

Slow Cooker Directions

1. Toss chicken with five-spice powder and red pepper flakes in small bowl. Heat peanut oil in large skillet. Add onion and chicken; cook and stir 5 minutes or until chicken is browned. Add mushrooms and garlic; cook and stir until chicken is no longer pink.

2. Stir ¼ cup broth into cornstarch in small bowl until smooth; set aside.

3. Place chicken mixture, remaining broth, bell pepper and soy sauce in slow cooker. Cover; cook on LOW 3½ hours or until peppers are tender.

4. Stir cornstarch mixture; add to slow cooker. Stir in green onions and sesame oil. Cook 30 to 45 minutes or until thickened. Ladle into bowls; serve with rice and sprinkle with cilantro, if desired.

Makes 4 to 6 servings

Slow Cooker Tuscan Beef Stew

1 can (10¾ ounces) CAMPBELL'S® Condensed Tomato Soup (Regular or Healthy Request®)

1 can (10½ ounces) CAMPBELL'S® Condensed Beef Broth

½ cup Burgundy wine or other dry red wine or water

1 teaspoon dried Italian seasoning, crushed

½ teaspoon garlic powder

1 can (about 14½ ounces) diced tomatoes with Italian herbs

3 large carrots, cut into 1-inch pieces (about 2 cups)

2 pounds beef for stew, cut into 1-inch pieces

2 cans (about 16 ounces each) white kidney beans (cannellini), rinsed and drained

Slow Cooker Directions

1. Stir the soup, broth, wine, Italian seasoning, garlic powder, tomatoes, carrots and beef in a 3½-quart slow cooker.

2. Cover and cook on LOW for 8 to 9 hours* or until the beef is fork-tender. Stir in the beans. Turn the heat to HIGH. Cook for 10 minutes or until the mixture is hot.   *Makes 8 servings*

*Or on HIGH for 4 to 5 hours.

Vegetable and Red Lentil Soup

1 can (about 14 ounces) vegetable broth

1 can (about 14 ounces) diced tomatoes

2 zucchini or yellow summer squash (or 1 of each), chopped

1 red or yellow bell pepper, chopped

½ cup thinly sliced carrots

½ cup dried red or brown lentils, rinsed and sorted

½ teaspoon *each* salt and sugar

¼ teaspoon black pepper

2 tablespoons chopped fresh basil or thyme

½ cup croutons (optional)

Slow Cooker Directions

1. Combine broth, tomatoes, zucchini, bell pepper, carrots, lentils, salt, sugar and black pepper in slow cooker. Cover; cook on LOW 8 hours or on HIGH 4 hours.

2. Ladle into shallow bowls; top with basil and croutons, if desired.   *Makes 4 servings*

Slow Cooker Tuscan Beef Stew

Chicken & Herb Dumplings

    2 pounds skinless, boneless chicken breasts and/or thighs, cut into 1-inch pieces
    5 medium carrots, cut into 1-inch pieces (about 2½ cups)
    4 stalks celery, cut into 1-inch pieces (about 2 cups)
    2 cups frozen whole kernel corn
 3½ cups SWANSON® Chicken Broth (Regular, Natural Goodness™ *or* Certified Organic)
   ¼ teaspoon ground black pepper
   ¼ cup all-purpose flour
   ½ cup water
    2 cups all-purpose baking mix
   ⅔ cup milk
    1 tablespoon chopped fresh rosemary leaves or 1 teaspoon dried rosemary leaves, crushed

Slow Cooker Directions

1. Stir the chicken, carrots, celery, corn, broth and black pepper in a 6-quart slow cooker.

2. Cover and cook on LOW for 7 to 8 hours* or until the chicken is cooked through.

3. Stir the flour and water in a small bowl until the mixture is smooth. Stir the flour mixture in the cooker. Turn the heat to HIGH. Cover and cook for 5 minutes or until the mixture boils and thickens.

4. Stir the baking mix, milk and rosemary in a medium bowl. Drop the batter by rounded tablespoonfuls over the chicken mixture. Tilt the lid to vent and cook on HIGH for 40 minutes or until the dumplings are cooked in the center.   *Makes 8 servings*

Or on HIGH for 4 to 5 hours.

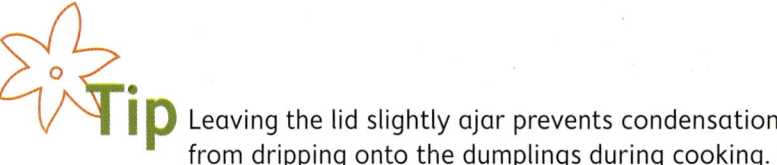

Tip Leaving the lid slightly ajar prevents condensation from dripping onto the dumplings during cooking.

Merlot Beef Chili with Horseradish Sour Cream

    2 tablespoons olive oil, divided
    1 pound boneless beef chuck roast, cut into $\frac{1}{2}$-inch pieces
    1 can (about 14 ounces) stewed tomatoes with Italian seasonings
    1 can ($10\frac{1}{2}$ ounces) condensed beef broth, undiluted
    1 can (8 ounces) tomato sauce
 $\frac{1}{2}$ cup chopped onion
 $\frac{1}{2}$ cup chopped green bell pepper
 $\frac{1}{4}$ cup Merlot or dry red wine
    1 tablespoon chili powder
    2 cloves garlic, minced
    2 teaspoons sugar
 $\frac{3}{4}$ teaspoon instant coffee granules
 $\frac{1}{2}$ teaspoon black pepper
    2 bay leaves
 $\frac{3}{4}$ cup sour cream
    3 tablespoons prepared horseradish
    1 teaspoon salt
      Cooked egg noodles (optional)

Slow Cooker Directions

1. Heat 1 tablespoon oil in large skillet over high heat. Add beef; cook and stir until browned on all sides. Transfer to slow cooker.

2. Stir in tomatoes, broth, tomato sauce, onion, bell pepper, wine, chili powder, garlic, sugar, coffee granules, black pepper and bay leaves. Cover; cook on LOW 12 hours or on HIGH 6 hours or until beef is very tender.

3. Meanwhile, combine sour cream, horseradish and salt in small bowl. Refrigerate in airtight container until needed.

4. Stir to break up large pieces of beef. Stir in remaining 1 tablespoon oil. Serve over egg noodles, if desired. Top with horseradish sour cream just before serving.   *Makes 4 servings*

Prep Time: 30 minutes
Cook Time: 12 hours (LOW) or 6 hours (HIGH)

Creamy Chicken Tortilla Soup

    1 small red pepper, chopped (about $1/2$ cup)
    1 small tomato, diced (about $1/2$ cup)
    1 can ($8^3/4$ ounces) whole kernel corn, drained
  $1/2$ pound skinless, boneless chicken breasts, cut into $1/2$-inch pieces
    1 can ($10^3/4$ ounces) CAMPBELL'S® Condensed Cream of Chicken Soup (Regular or 98% Fat Free)
 $1^1/2$ cups water
    1 teaspoon ground cumin
  $1/2$ teaspoon ground coriander
  $1/2$ teaspoon garlic powder
  $1/2$ teaspoon chili powder
    1 can (about 4 ounces) chopped green chiles
  $1/4$ teaspoon chopped jalapeño pepper (optional)
    2 corn tortillas (6 inch), cut into strips
  $1/2$ cup shredded Cheddar cheese
  $1/4$ cup chopped fresh cilantro leaves

Slow Cooker Directions

1. Stir the pepper, tomato, corn and chicken in a $3^1/2$-quart slow cooker.

2. Stir the soup, water, cumin, coriander, garlic powder, chili powder, chiles and jalapeño pepper, if desired, in a small bowl. Pour over the chicken mixture.

3. Cover and cook on LOW for 4 to 5 hours* or until the chicken is cooked through.

4. Stir in the tortillas, cheese and cilantro. Cover and cook for 30 minutes. Serve with additional cheese, if desired.   *Makes 4 servings*

Or on HIGH for 2 to $2^1/2$ hours.

Prep Time: 10 minutes
Cook Time: 4 hours, 30 minutes

Pork and Anaheim Stew

             2 tablespoons olive oil, divided
1½ pounds boneless pork shoulder, trimmed of fat and cut into ½-inch pieces
             6 Anaheim peppers, halved lengthwise, seeded and sliced
             4 cloves garlic, minced
             1 pound tomatillos, papery skins removed, rinsed and chopped
             2 cups chopped onions
             1 can (about 15 ounces) yellow hominy, rinsed and drained
             1 can (about 14 ounces) chicken broth
             2 teaspoons chili powder
1½ teaspoons sugar
             1 teaspoon ground cumin
             1 teaspoon dried oregano
             1 teaspoon liquid smoke
             ½ teaspoon salt

Slow Cooker Directions

1. Heat 1 tablespoon oil in large skillet over medium-high heat. Brown pork in batches. Transfer to slow cooker.

2. Add Anaheim peppers to same skillet; cook and stir 5 minutes or until edges are very brown. Add garlic; cook and stir 30 seconds. Transfer to slow cooker.

3. Stir in tomatillos, onions, hominy, broth, chili powder, sugar, cumin and oregano. Cover; cook on LOW 10 hours or on HIGH 5 hours.

4. Stir in remaining 1 tablespoon oil, liquid smoke and salt.   *Makes 4 to 6 servings*

Prep Time: 30 minutes
Cook Time: 10 hours (LOW) or 5 hours (HIGH)

Country Chicken Chowder

       2 tablespoons butter
$1\frac{1}{2}$ pounds chicken tenders, cut into $\frac{1}{2}$-inch pieces
       2 onions, chopped
       2 stalks celery, sliced
       2 carrots, sliced
       2 cups frozen corn
       2 cans ($10\frac{3}{4}$ ounces each) condensed cream of potato soup, undiluted
$1\frac{1}{2}$ cups chicken broth
       1 teaspoon dried dill weed
   $\frac{1}{2}$ cup half-and-half

Slow Cooker Directions

1. Melt butter in large skillet over medium-high heat. Add chicken; cook until browned. Transfer to slow cooker. Top with onions, celery, carrots, corn, soups, broth and dill weed.

2. Cover; cook on LOW 3 to 4 hours. Turn off heat; stir in half-and-half. Cover; let stand 5 minutes or until heated through.   *Makes 8 servings*

Lentil Soup with Beef

       3 cans ($10\frac{1}{2}$ ounces each) CAMPBELL'S® Condensed French Onion Soup
       1 soup can water
       3 stalks celery, sliced (about $1\frac{1}{2}$ cups)
       3 large carrots, sliced (about $1\frac{1}{2}$ cups)
$1\frac{1}{2}$ cups dried lentils
       1 can (about $14\frac{1}{2}$ ounces) diced tomatoes
       1 teaspoon dried thyme leaves, crushed
       3 cloves garlic, minced
       2 pounds beef for stew, cut into 1-inch pieces

Slow Cooker Directions

1. Stir the soup, water, celery, carrots, lentils, tomatoes, thyme, garlic and beef in a 5-quart slow cooker. Season as desired.

2. Cover and cook on LOW for 7 to 8 hours* or until the beef is fork-tender.

Makes 8 servings

*Or on HIGH for 4 to 5 hours.

Country Chicken Chowder

Pasta Fagioli Soup

2 cans (about 14 ounces each) beef or vegetable broth
1 can (about 15 ounces) Great Northern beans, rinsed and drained
1 can (about 14 ounces) diced tomatoes
2 zucchini, quartered lengthwise and sliced
1 tablespoon olive oil
1½ teaspoons minced garlic
½ teaspoon dried basil
½ teaspoon dried oregano
½ cup uncooked tubetti, ditalini or small shell pasta
½ cup garlic seasoned croutons
½ cup grated Asiago or Romano cheese
3 tablespoons chopped fresh basil or Italian parsley (optional)

Slow Cooker Directions

1. Combine broth, beans, tomatoes, zucchini, oil, garlic, dried basil and oregano in slow cooker; mix well. Cover; cook on LOW 3 to 4 hours.

2. Stir in pasta. Cover; cook on LOW 1 hour or until pasta is tender.

3. Serve soup with croutons and cheese. Garnish with fresh basil.   *Makes 5 to 6 servings*

Prep Time: 12 minutes
Cook Time: 4 to 5 hours

**Tip** Only small pasta varieties like tubetti, ditalini or small shells should be used in this recipe. The low heat of the slow cooker is not enough to cook larger pasta shapes completely.

Creamy Farmhouse Chicken and Garden Soup

½ package (16 ounces) frozen stir-fry vegetables
1 cup frozen corn, thawed
1 zucchini, sliced
1 can (about 14 ounces) chicken broth
4 bone-in chicken thighs, skinned
½ teaspoon minced garlic
½ teaspoon dried thyme
2 ounces uncooked egg noodles
1 cup half-and-half
½ cup frozen green peas
2 tablespoons chopped fresh Italian parsley
2 tablespoons butter
1 teaspoon salt
½ teaspoon black pepper

Slow Cooker Directions

1. Combine stir-fry vegetables, corn and zucchini in slow cooker. Add broth, chicken, garlic and thyme. Cover; cook on HIGH 3 to 4 hours or until chicken is no longer pink in center. Remove chicken; cool slightly.

2. Add noodles to slow cooker. Cover; cook 20 minutes or until noodles are almost tender.

3. Meanwhile, debone and chop chicken. Return to slow cooker. Stir in half-and-half, peas, parsley, butter, salt and pepper. Let stand 5 minutes before serving.   *Makes 2 to 4 servings*

Prep Time: 15 minutes
Cook Time: 3 to 4 hours, plus 25 minutes

Beef and Eggplant Stew

1 teaspoon olive oil
1 small eggplant, trimmed and cut into 1-inch chunks
2 cups shiitake or cremini mushrooms, quartered
1 can (about 14 ounces) diced tomatoes
½ pound beef top round steak, cut into 1-inch pieces
1 onion, chopped
1 cup beef broth
  Grated peel of 1 lemon
1 clove garlic, minced
½ teaspoon salt
⅓ teaspoon ground cumin
¼ teaspoon red pepper flakes
¼ teaspoon ground cinnamon
⅛ teaspoon black pepper

Slow Cooker Directions

1. Heat oil in large nonstick skillet over medium-high heat. Add eggplant; cook 3 to 5 minutes or until lightly browned on all sides, stirring frequently. Transfer to slow cooker.

2. Stir in mushrooms, tomatoes, steak, onion, broth, lemon peel, garlic, salt, cumin, red pepper flakes, cinnamon and black pepper. Cover; cook on LOW 6 hours.   *Makes 2 to 4 servings*

Tip Shiitake are wild mushrooms from Japan that are easily cultivated. They have brown caps, a firm texture and thin tough stems, which are usually trimmed away. Their woodsy aroma and rich, smoky mushroom flavor contribute to their popularity.

FAMILY FAVORITES

Chinese Pork Tenderloin

2 pork tenderloins (about 2 pounds total)
1 green bell pepper, cut into $\frac{1}{2}$-inch dice
1 red bell pepper, cut into $\frac{1}{2}$-inch dice
1 onion, thinly sliced
2 carrots, thinly sliced
1 jar (15 ounces) sweet and sour sauce
1 tablespoon soy sauce
$\frac{1}{2}$ teaspoon hot pepper sauce
   Hot cooked white rice
   Chopped fresh cilantro or Italian parsley (optional)

Slow Cooker Directions

1. Cut pork into 1-inch cubes and place in slow cooker.

2. Add bell peppers, onion, carrots, sweet and sour sauce, soy sauce and hot pepper sauce; stir to combine.

3. Cover; cook on LOW 6 to 7 hours or on HIGH 4 to 5 hours. Stir just before serving. Serve over rice and sprinkle with cilantro, if desired. *Makes 8 servings*

Prep Time: 15 minutes
Cook Time: 6 to 7 hours (LOW) or 4 to 5 hours (HIGH)

Chicken Vesuvio

          3 tablespoons all-purpose flour
1½ teaspoons dried oregano
          1 teaspoon salt
       ½ teaspoon black pepper
          1 whole chicken (3 to 4 pounds), cut up
          2 tablespoons olive oil
          4 baking potatoes, cut into wedges
          2 onions, cut into thin wedges
          4 cloves garlic, minced
       ¼ cup chicken broth
       ¼ cup dry white wine
       ¼ cup chopped fresh Italian parsley
             Lemon wedges (optional)

Slow Cooker Directions

1. Combine flour, oregano, salt and pepper in large resealable food storage bag. Add several pieces of chicken to bag; shake to coat. Repeat with remaining chicken.

2. Heat oil in large skillet over medium heat. Add chicken; cook 10 to 12 minutes or until browned on all sides, turning occasionally.

3. Place potatoes, onions and garlic in slow cooker. Add broth and wine. Top with chicken pieces; pour pan juices from skillet over chicken. Cover; cook on LOW 6 to 7 hours or on HIGH 3 to 3½ hours or until chicken is cooked through and potatoes are tender.

4. Serve chicken and vegetables with juices from slow cooker. Sprinkle with parsley. Serve with lemon wedges, if desired. *Makes 4 to 6 servings*

Spinach and Ricotta Stuffed Shells

1 package (16 ounces) jumbo pasta shells
1 package (15 ounces) ricotta cheese
1 package (10 ounces) frozen chopped spinach, thawed and squeezed dry
$\frac{1}{2}$ cup grated Parmesan cheese
1 egg, lightly beaten
1 clove garlic, minced
$\frac{1}{2}$ teaspoon salt
1 jar (26 ounces) marinara sauce
$\frac{1}{2}$ cup (2 ounces) shredded mozzarella cheese
1 teaspoon olive oil

Slow Cooker Directions

1. Cook pasta shells according to package directions until almost tender. Drain well; set aside.

2. Stir together ricotta cheese, spinach, Parmesan cheese, egg, garlic and salt in large bowl.

3. Pour $\frac{1}{4}$ cup marinara sauce in bottom of slow cooker. Spoon 2 to 3 tablespoons ricotta mixture into 1 pasta shell and place in bottom of slow cooker. Repeat with enough additional shells to cover bottom of slow cooker. Top with another $\frac{1}{4}$ cup marinara sauce. Repeat with remaining pasta shells and filling. Top with any remaining marinara sauce and sprinkle with mozzarella cheese. Drizzle with oil.

4. Cover; cook on HIGH 3 to 4 hours or until mozzarella cheese is melted and sauce is heated through. *Makes 4 to 6 servings*

Prep Time: 45 minutes
Cook Time: 3 to 4 hours

Shredded Pork Burritos with Green Chile Sauce

1 tablespoon vegetable oil
1 large onion, chopped (about 1 cup)
4 cloves garlic, minced
2 jars (16 ounces each) PACE® Chunky Salsa
1 cup water
1 medium red pepper, chopped (about 1 cup)
8 green onions, chopped (about 1 cup)
1 bunch fresh cilantro leaves, chopped (about 1 cup)
¼ cup lemon pepper seasoning
¼ cup ground cumin
¼ cup chili powder
1 tablespoon lime juice
1 (4-pound) boneless pork loin roast, netted or tied
1 can (4 ounces) diced green chiles, drained
12 flour tortillas (10 inch), warmed
2 cups shredded Monterey Jack cheese (about 8 ounces)

Slow Cooker Directions

1. Heat the oil in a 12-inch skillet over medium heat. Add the onion and garlic and cook until they're tender. Stir the salsa, water, red pepper, green onions, cilantro, lemon pepper, cumin, chili powder and lime juice in the skillet.

2. Place the pork into a 5-quart slow cooker. Pour the salsa mixture over the pork.

3. Cover and cook on LOW for 8 to 9 hours* or until the pork is fork-tender.

4. Remove the pork from the cooker to a cutting board and let stand for 10 minutes. Using 2 forks, shred the pork.

5. Spoon **5 cups** salsa mixture into a 2-quart saucepan. Stir in the chiles and cook over medium-high heat to a boil. Reduce the heat to low. Cook and stir for 15 minutes or until the mixture thickens.

6. Spoon **1 cup** pork down the center of **each** tortilla. Top **each** with **2 tablespoons** green chile sauce. Fold the sides of the tortillas over the filling and then fold up the ends to enclose the filling. Divide the remaining green chile sauce and the cheese over the burritos.

Makes 12 burritos

Or on HIGH for 4 to 5 hours.

Sweet and Sour Shrimp

1 can (16 ounces) sliced peaches in syrup, undrained
½ cup chopped green onions
½ cup chopped red bell pepper
½ cup chopped green bell pepper
½ cup chopped celery
⅓ cup vegetable broth
¼ cup light soy sauce
2 tablespoons rice wine vinegar
2 tablespoons dark sesame oil
1 teaspoon red pepper flakes
1 package (6 ounces) snow peas
1 pound cooked medium shrimp
1 cup cherry tomatoes, cut into halves
½ cup walnut pieces, toasted
    Hot cooked rice

Slow Cooker Directions

1. Place peaches, green onions, bell peppers, celery, broth, soy sauce, vinegar, sesame oil and red pepper flakes in slow cooker. Cover; cook on LOW 3 to 4 hours or on HIGH 2 to 3 hours or until vegetables are tender. Stir well.

2. *Turn slow cooker to HIGH.* Add snow peas. Cook 15 minutes.

3. Add shrimp, tomatoes and walnuts. Cook 5 minutes or until shrimp are heated through. Serve over rice.   *Makes 4 to 6 servings*

Prep Time: 15 to 20 minutes
Cook Time: 3 to 4 hours (LOW) or 2 to 3 hours (HIGH), plus 20 minutes

Chicken Marsala with Fettuccine

    4 boneless skinless chicken breasts
      Salt and black pepper
    1 tablespoon vegetable oil
    1 onion, chopped
  ½ cup marsala wine
    2 packages (6 ounces each) sliced cremini mushrooms
  ½ cup chicken broth
    2 teaspoons Worcestershire sauce
  ½ cup whipping cream
    2 tablespoons cornstarch
    8 ounces uncooked fettuccine
    2 tablespoons chopped fresh Italian parsley

Slow Cooker Directions

1. Lightly coat slow cooker with nonstick cooking spray. Place chicken in slow cooker; season with salt and pepper.

2. Heat oil in large skillet over medium heat. Add onion; cook and stir 2 minutes or until translucent. Add marsala; cook 2 to 3 minutes or until slightly thickened. Stir in mushrooms, broth and Worcestershire sauce. Pour mixture over chicken. Cover; cook on HIGH 1½ to 1¾ hours.

3. Transfer chicken to cutting board; cover and keep warm. Stir cream into cornstarch in small bowl until smooth; stir into cooking liquid. Cover; cook 15 minutes or until thickened. Season with salt and pepper.

4. Meanwhile, cook pasta according to package directions. Drain well; transfer to large serving bowl. Slice chicken and place on pasta. Top with sauce and sprinkle with parsley.

Makes 6 servings

Prep Time: 10 minutes
Cook Time: 1½ to 1¾ hours, plus 15 minutes

Slow-Cooked Taco Shredded Beef

1 can (10¾ ounces) CAMPBELL'S® Condensed French Onion Soup
1 tablespoon chili powder
½ teaspoon ground cumin
1 (2-pound) boneless beef chuck roast
2 tablespoons finely chopped fresh cilantro leaves
16 taco shells
1 cup shredded Cheddar cheese (about 4 ounces)
    Shredded lettuce
    Sour cream

Slow Cooker Directions

1. Stir the soup, chili powder and cumin in a 4-quart slow cooker. Add the beef and turn to coat.

2. Cover and cook on LOW for 6 to 7 hours* or until the beef is fork-tender.

3. Remove the beef from the cooker to a cutting board and let stand for 10 minutes. Using 2 forks, shred the beef. Return the beef to the cooker. Stir the cilantro in the cooker.

4. Spoon about ¼ **cup** beef mixture into **each** taco shell. Top **each** with **about 1 tablespoon** cheese. Top with the lettuce and the sour cream.   *Makes 16 tacos*

Or on HIGH for 4 to 5 hours.

Prep Time: 10 minutes
Cook Time: 6 to 7 hours
Stand Time: 10 minutes

Slow-Cooked Taco Shredded Beef

Italian Sausage and Peppers

3 cups diced red, green and yellow bell peppers
1 onion, cut into thin wedges
3 cloves garlic, minced
4 links hot or mild Italian sausage (about 1 pound)
1 cup pasta or marinara sauce
¼ cup red wine
1 tablespoon cornstarch
1 tablespoon water
Hot cooked spaghetti
¼ cup shredded Parmesan or Romano cheese

Slow Cooker Directions

1. Lightly coat slow cooker with cooking spray. Place bell peppers, onion and garlic in slow cooker. Arrange sausage over vegetables. Combine pasta sauce and wine in small bowl; pour over sausage. Cover; cook on LOW 8 to 9 hours or on HIGH 4 to 5 hours.

2. Transfer sausage to serving platter. Cover with foil; keep warm. Let liquid in slow cooker stand 5 minutes. Skim off fat.

3. *Turn slow cooker to HIGH.* Stir water into cornstarch in small bowl until smooth. Add to slow cooker; stir until blended. Cook 15 minutes or until sauce is thickened, stirring once. Serve sauce over spaghetti and sausage; top with Parmesan cheese. *Makes 4 servings*

Tip Wines of all sorts are used in cooking. Special cooking wines available in supermarkets are not recommended because they are often inferior in quality and contain lots of added salt. However, there is no need to use fine vintages for cooking. Leftover wine that is no longer good for drinking after a day or two is perfectly fine for cooking.

Asian Beef with Broccoli

1½ **pounds boneless beef chuck steak, about 1½ inches thick, thinly sliced***
  1 **can (10½ ounces) beef consommé**
½ **cup oyster sauce**
  2 **tablespoons cornstarch**
  1 **bag (16 ounces) fresh broccoli florets**
    Hot cooked rice
    Sesame seeds (optional)

*To make slicing steak easier, place in freezer for 30 minutes before slicing.

Slow Cooker Directions

1. Place steak in slow cooker. Pour in consommé and oyster sauce. Cover; cook on LOW 6 to 8 hours or on HIGH 3 hours.

2. *Turn slow cooker to HIGH.* Stir 2 tablespoons cooking liquid into cornstarch in small bowl until smooth. Add to slow cooker; stir until blended. Cook, uncovered, 15 minutes or until thickened.

3. Cook broccoli according to package directions. Stir into slow cooker. Serve over rice. Garnish with sesame seeds. *Makes 4 to 6 servings*

Slow Cooker Sloppy Joes

  1 **envelope LIPTON® RECIPE SECRETS® Onion Soup Mix**
1½ **pounds ground beef, browned and drained**
  1 **cup water**
  1 **cup ketchup**
  2 **tablespoons firmly packed brown sugar**
  6 **hamburger buns**

Slow Cooker Directions

1. In slow cooker, combine LIPTON® RECIPE SECRETS® Onion Soup Mix with rest of ingredients, except hamburger buns.

2. Cook, covered, on LOW 4 to 6 hours or on HIGH 2 to 3 hours. Serve on hamburger buns. *Makes 6 servings*

Asian Beef with Broccoli

COUNTRY CLASSICS

Forty-Clove Chicken

   1 whole chicken (3 to 4 pounds), cut up
     Salt and black pepper
   1 to 2 tablespoons olive oil
 ¼ cup dry white wine
   2 tablespoons chopped fresh Italian parsley *or* 2 teaspoons dried parsley
   2 tablespoons dry vermouth
   2 teaspoons dried basil
   1 teaspoon dried oregano
     Pinch red pepper flakes
  40 cloves garlic (about 2 bulbs), peeled
   4 stalks celery, sliced
     Juice and peel of 1 lemon

Slow Cooker Directions

1. Remove skin from chicken. Sprinkle chicken with salt and pepper.

2. Heat oil in large skillet over medium heat. Add chicken; brown on all sides. Transfer to platter.

3. Combine wine, parsley, vermouth, basil, oregano and red pepper flakes in large bowl. Add garlic and celery; coat well. Transfer garlic and celery to slow cooker with slotted spoon.

4. Add chicken to herb mixture; coat well. Place chicken on top of vegetable mixture in slow cooker; pour any remaining herb mixture over chicken. Sprinkle lemon juice and peel over chicken. Cover; cook on LOW 6 hours. *Makes 4 to 6 servings*

Favorite Beef Stew

        3 carrots, halved and cut into 1-inch pieces
        3 stalks celery, cut into 1-inch pieces
        2 large potatoes, peeled and cut into ½-inch pieces
    1½ cups chopped onions
        3 cloves garlic, chopped
    4½ teaspoons Worcestershire sauce
      ¾ teaspoon dried thyme
      ¾ teaspoon dried basil
      ½ teaspoon black pepper
        1 bay leaf
        2 pounds beef stew meat (1-inch pieces)
        1 can (about 14 ounces) diced tomatoes
        1 can (about 14 ounces) beef broth
      ½ cup cold water
      ¼ cup all-purpose flour

Slow Cooker Directions

1. Layer ingredients in slow cooker in the following order: carrots, celery, potatoes, onions, garlic, Worcestershire sauce, thyme, basil, pepper, bay leaf, beef, tomatoes and broth.

2. Cover; cook on LOW 8 to 9 hours.

3. Remove beef and vegetables to large serving bowl; cover and keep warm. Remove and discard bay leaf.

4. *Turn slow cooker to HIGH.* Stir water into flour in small bowl until smooth. Add ½ cup cooking liquid; mix well. Stir flour mixture into slow cooker. Cover; cook 15 minutes or until thickened. Pour sauce over meat and vegetables. Serve immediately.   *Makes 6 to 8 servings*

Slow Cooker Chicken and Dressing

> 4 boneless skinless chicken breasts
> Salt and black pepper
> 4 slices Swiss cheese
> 2 cans (10¾ ounces each) condensed cream of chicken, celery or mushroom soup, undiluted
> 1 can (about 14 ounces) chicken broth
> 3 cups herb-seasoned stuffing mix
> ½ cup (1 stick) butter, melted

Slow Cooker Directions

1. Place chicken in slow cooker. Season with salt and pepper.

2. Top each breast with cheese slice. Add soup and broth. Sprinkle stuffing mix over top; pour melted butter over all. Cover; cook on LOW 6 to 8 hours or on HIGH 3 to 4 hours.

Makes 4 servings

Simply Satisfying Meat Loaf

> 1½ pounds ground beef
> ¾ cup milk
> ⅔ cup plain dry bread crumbs
> 2 eggs, beaten
> 2 tablespoons minced onion
> 1 teaspoon salt
> ½ teaspoon ground sage
> ½ cup ketchup
> 2 tablespoons packed brown sugar
> 1 teaspoon dry mustard

Slow Cooker Directions

1. Combine beef, milk, bread crumbs, eggs, onion, salt and sage in large bowl; shape into ball. Place in slow cooker. Cover; cook on LOW 5 to 6 hours.

2. *Turn slow cooker to HIGH.* Combine ketchup, brown sugar and mustard in small bowl. Pour over meat loaf. Cover; cook 15 minutes.

Makes 6 servings

Slow Cooker Chicken and Dressing

Country Captain Chicken

4 boneless skinless chicken thighs
2 tablespoons all-purpose flour
2 tablespoons vegetable oil, divided
1 cup chopped green bell pepper
1 onion, chopped
1 stalk celery, chopped
1 clove garlic, minced
¼ cup chicken broth
2 cups canned crushed tomatoes or diced fresh tomatoes
½ cup golden raisins
1½ teaspoons curry powder
1 teaspoon salt
¼ teaspoon paprika
¼ teaspoon black pepper
2 cups hot cooked rice

Slow Cooker Directions

1. Coat chicken with flour; set aside. Heat 1 tablespoon oil in large skillet over medium-high heat. Add bell pepper, onion, celery and garlic. Cook and stir 5 minutes or until vegetables are tender. Transfer to slow cooker.

2. Heat remaining 1 tablespoon oil in same skillet over medium-high heat. Add chicken; cook 5 minutes per side or until browned. Transfer to slow cooker.

3. Pour broth into skillet. Cook and stir over medium-high heat, stirring to scrape up browned bits from bottom of skillet. Pour liquid into slow cooker.

4. Add tomatoes, raisins, curry powder, salt, paprika and black pepper. Cover; cook on LOW 3 hours. Serve chicken and sauce over rice.   *Makes 2 to 4 servings*

No-Fuss Macaroni & Cheese

    2 cups (about 8 ounces) uncooked elbow macaroni
    4 ounces pasteurized processed cheese, cubed
    1 cup (4 ounces) shredded mild Cheddar cheese
    ½ teaspoon salt
    ⅛ teaspoon black pepper
    1½ cups milk

Slow Cooker Directions

Combine macaroni, cheeses, salt and pepper in slow cooker. Pour milk over top. Cover; cook on LOW 2 to 3 hours, stirring after 20 to 30 minutes.   *Makes 6 to 8 servings*

Note: As with all macaroni and cheese dishes, the cheese sauce thickens and begins to dry out as it sits. If it becomes too dry, stir in a little extra milk. Do not cook longer than 4 hours.

Prep Time: 10 minutes
Cook Time: 2 to 3 hours

Red Beans and Rice with Ham

    1 package (16 ounces) dried red beans, rinsed and sorted
    1 pound smoked beef sausage, sliced
    1 ham slice (about 8 ounces), cubed
    1 onion, diced
    2½ to 3 cups water
    1 teaspoon Mexican (adobo) seasoning with pepper
    ⅛ teaspoon ground red pepper
      Hot cooked rice

Slow Cooker Directions

1. Place beans in large bowl; cover completely with water. Soak 6 to 8 hours or overnight. Drain beans; discard water.

2. Place beans in slow cooker. Add sausage, ham, onion, water (2½ cups for LOW or 3 cups for HIGH), seasoning and red pepper.

3. Cover; cook on LOW 7 to 8 hours or on HIGH 3 to 4 hours or until beans are tender, stirring every 2 hours. Serve over rice.   *Makes 6 servings*

Beef with Sweet Potatoes and Apples

    1 boneless beef chuck shoulder roast (2 pounds)
    1 can (40 ounces) sweet potatoes, drained
    2 onions, sliced
    2 apples, cored and sliced
  1/2 cup beef broth
    2 cloves garlic, minced
    1 teaspoon salt
    1 teaspoon dried thyme, divided
  3/4 teaspoon black pepper, divided
    1 tablespoon cornstarch
  1/4 teaspoon ground cinnamon
    2 tablespoons water

Slow Cooker Directions

1. Trim and discard fat from beef. Cut beef into 2-inch pieces. Place beef, sweet potatoes, onions, apples, broth, garlic, salt, 1/2 teaspoon thyme and 1/2 teaspoon pepper in slow cooker. Cover; cook on LOW 8 to 9 hours.

2. Transfer beef, sweet potatoes and apples to platter; keep warm. Let liquid stand 15 minutes; skim off fat.

3. *Turn slow cooker to HIGH.* Stir together cornstarch, remaining 1/2 teaspoon thyme, 1/4 teaspoon pepper, cinnamon and water in small bowl until smooth; stir into cooking liquid. Cook 15 minutes or until thickened. Serve sauce with beef, sweet potatoes and apples.

Makes 6 servings

Prep Time: 20 minutes
Cook Time: 8 to 9 hours, plus 15 minutes

Cream Cheese Chicken with Broccoli

4 pounds boneless skinless chicken breasts, cut into ¹/₂-inch pieces
1 tablespoon olive oil
1 package (1 ounce) Italian salad dressing mix
   Nonstick cooking spray
2 cups sliced mushrooms
1 cup chopped onion
1 can (10³/₄ ounces) condensed cream of chicken soup, undiluted
1 bag (10 ounces) frozen broccoli florets
1 package (8 ounces) cream cheese, cubed
¹/₄ cup dry sherry
   Hot cooked pasta (optional)

Slow Cooker Directions

1. Toss chicken with oil. Sprinkle with salad dressing mix. Place in slow cooker. Cover; cook on LOW 3 hours.

2. Spray large nonstick skillet with cooking spray; heat over medium heat. Add mushrooms and onion; cook 5 minutes or until onions are tender, stirring occasionally.

3. Add soup, broccoli, cream cheese and sherry to saucepan; cook and stir until heated through. Transfer to slow cooker. Cover; cook on LOW 1 hour. Serve over pasta, if desired.

Makes 10 to 12 servings

Tip Fortified wines are wines that have brandy or other alcohol added to them for the purpose of increasing their alcoholic content. Examples include sherry, Madeira, marsala and port.

Yankee Pot Roast and Vegetables

    1 beef chuck pot roast (2½ pounds)
      Salt and black pepper
    3 unpeeled baking potatoes (about 1 pound), cut into quarters
    2 carrots, cut into ¾-inch slices
    2 stalks celery, cut into ¾-inch slices
    1 onion, sliced
    1 parsnip, cut into ¾-inch slices
    2 bay leaves
    1 teaspoon dried rosemary
  ½ teaspoon dried thyme
  ½ cup beef broth

Slow Cooker Directions

1. Trim and discard excess fat from beef. Cut beef into serving-size pieces; season with salt and pepper.

2. Combine potatoes, carrots, celery, onion, parsnip, bay leaves, rosemary and thyme in slow cooker. Top with beef. Pour broth over beef. Cover; cook on LOW 8½ to 9 hours or until beef is fork-tender.

3. Transfer beef and vegetables to serving platter. Remove and discard bay leaves.

Makes 10 to 12 servings

Note: To make gravy, ladle the juices into a 2-cup measure; let stand 5 minutes. Skim off and discard fat. Measure remaining juices and heat to a boil in small saucepan. For each cup of juice, stir ¼ cup cold water into 2 tablespoons flour in small bowl until smooth. Add mixture to boiling juices; cook and stir constantly 1 minute or until thickened.

Prep Time: 10 minutes
Cook Time: 8½ to 9 hours

Cajun-Style Country Ribs

2 cups baby carrots
1 onion, coarsely chopped
1 green bell pepper, cut into 1-inch pieces
1 red bell pepper, cut into 1-inch pieces
2 teaspoons minced garlic
2 tablespoons Cajun or Creole seasoning, divided
3½ to 4 pounds pork country-style spareribs
1 can (about 14 ounces) stewed tomatoes, undrained
2 tablespoons water
1 tablespoon cornstarch
Hot cooked rice

Slow Cooker Directions

1. Combine carrots, onion, bell peppers, garlic and 2 teaspoons seasoning in slow cooker; mix well.

2. Trim excess fat from ribs; cut into individual ribs. Sprinkle with 1 tablespoon seasoning; place in slow cooker. Pour tomatoes over ribs. Cover; cook on LOW 6 to 8 hours.

3. Remove ribs and vegetables from cooking liquid to serving platter. Let liquid stand 15 minutes; skim off fat.

4. *Turn slow cooker to HIGH.* Stir water into cornstarch and remaining 1 teaspoon Cajun seasoning in small bowl until smooth. Add to slow cooker; stir until well blended. Cook, uncovered, 15 minutes or until sauce is thickened. Return ribs and vegetables to sauce; carefully stir to coat. Serve with rice.   *Makes 6 to 8 servings*

Prep Time: 15 minutes
Cook Time: 6 to 8 hours, plus 15 minutes

Classic Pot Roast

1 tablespoon vegetable oil
1 beef chuck shoulder roast (3 to 4 pounds)
6 medium potatoes, halved
6 carrots, sliced
2 onions, quartered
2 stalks celery, sliced
1 can (about 14 ounces) diced tomatoes
  Salt and black pepper
  Dried oregano
  Water
1½ to 2 tablespoons all-purpose flour

Slow Cooker Directions

1. Heat oil in large skillet over medium-low heat. Add roast; brown on all sides. Transfer to slow cooker.

2. Add potatoes, carrots, onions, celery and tomatoes. Season with salt, pepper and oregano. Add enough water to cover bottom of slow cooker by about ½ inch.

3. Cover; cook on LOW 8 to 10 hours. Remove roast to platter. Let stand 15 minutes.

4. Transfer juices to small saucepan. Whisk in flour until smooth. Cook and stir over medium heat until thickened. Slice roast and serve with gravy. *Makes 6 to 8 servings*

Cook Time: 8 to 10 hours

Asian Pork Ribs with Spicy Noodles

1 can (about 14 ounces) beef broth

½ cup water

¼ cup rice wine vinegar

1 ounce (2-inch piece) ginger, peeled and grated

1 cup (about 1 ounce) dried sliced shiitake mushrooms

¼ teaspoon red pepper flakes

1 tablespoon Chinese five-spice powder

1 tablespoon dark sesame oil

1 teaspoon ground ginger

1 teaspoon chili powder

2 full racks pork baby back ribs (about 4 pounds total)

¾ cup hoisin sauce, divided

1 pound (16 ounces) thin rice noodles or spaghetti, cooked according to package directions

¼ cup thinly sliced green onions

¼ cup chopped fresh cilantro

Slow Cooker Directions

1. Stir together broth, water, vinegar, grated ginger, shiitake mushrooms and red pepper flakes in slow cooker.

2. Stir together five-spice powder, sesame oil, ground ginger and chili powder in small bowl to form a paste. Cut rib racks in half; dry with paper towels. Rub all surfaces with spice paste; brush with half of hoisin sauce.

3. Place ribs in slow cooker with broth mixture (do not stir). Cover; cook on LOW 8 to 10 hours or on HIGH 5 to 6 hours or until meat is tender when pierced with fork. Transfer ribs to platter; brush lightly with remaining hoisin sauce. Cover; keep warm. Skim off any fat from cooking liquid.

4. Place noodles in shallow bowls. Ladle some cooking liquid over noodles; sprinkle with green onions and cilantro. Slice ribs; serve over noodles.   *Makes 4 servings*

Prep Time: 20 minutes
Cook Time: 8 to 10 hours (LOW) or 5 to 6 hours (HIGH)

Ham and Sage Stuffed Cornish Hens

> 1 cup plus 3 tablespoons sliced celery, divided
> 1 cup sliced leek
> 2 tablespoons butter, divided
> ¼ cup finely diced onion
> ¼ cup diced smoked ham or prosciutto
> 1 cup herb-seasoned stuffing mix
> 1 cup chicken broth
> 1 tablespoon finely chopped fresh sage *or* 1 teaspoon ground sage
> 4 Cornish hens (about 1½ pounds each)
>   Salt and black pepper

Slow Cooker Directions

1. Lightly coat slow cooker with nonstick cooking spray. Add 1 cup celery and leek.

2. Melt 1 tablespoon butter in large nonstick skillet over medium heat. Add remaining 3 tablespoons celery, onion and ham. Cook 5 minutes or until onion is translucent, stirring frequently. Stir in stuffing mix, broth and sage. Transfer mixture to medium bowl; set aside.

3. Rinse hens and pat dry; sprinkle with salt and pepper. Spoon stuffing into cavities; tie drumsticks together with kitchen twine.

4. Melt remaining 1 tablespoon butter in same skillet over medium-high heat. Add 2 hens; cook until browned on all sides, turning occasionally. Transfer to slow cooker. Repeat with remaining hens.

5. Cover; cook on LOW 5 to 6 hours or on HIGH 3 to 4 hours.

6. To serve, remove and discard twine. Place hens on serving platter with vegetables; spoon broth over hens.

Makes 4 servings

Prep Time: 45 minutes
Cook Time: 5 to 6 hours (LOW) or 3 to 4 hours (HIGH)

Citrus Pork with Pineapple Salsa

1½ teaspoons ground cumin
½ teaspoon black pepper
¼ teaspoon salt
1½ pounds center-cut pork loin
1 tablespoon vegetable oil
2 cans (8 ounces each) pineapple tidbits* in juice, drained and 4 tablespoons juice reserved
2 tablespoons lemon juice, divided
1 teaspoon grated lemon peel
½ cup finely chopped orange or red bell pepper
2 tablespoons finely chopped red onion
1 tablespoon chopped fresh cilantro or mint
½ teaspoon grated fresh ginger
⅛ teaspoon red pepper flakes (optional)

*If tidbits are unavailable, purchase pineapple chunks and coarsely chop.

Slow Cooker Directions

1. Lightly coat slow cooker with nonstick cooking spray. Combine cumin, black pepper and salt in small bowl. Rub evenly onto pork. Heat oil in medium skillet over medium-high heat. Brown pork 1 to 2 minutes per side. Transfer to slow cooker.

2. Spoon 2 tablespoons reserved pineapple juice and 1 tablespoon lemon juice over pork. Cover; cook on LOW 2 hours or on HIGH 1 hour or until meat thermometer registers 160°F and pork is barely pink in center. *Do not overcook.*

3. Meanwhile, combine pineapple, remaining 2 tablespoons pineapple juice, remaining 1 tablespoon lemon juice, lemon peel, bell pepper, onion, cilantro, ginger and red pepper flakes, if desired, in medium bowl. Toss gently until blended.

4. Transfer pork to serving platter. Let stand 10 minutes before slicing. Pour juices evenly over pork. Serve with salsa. *Makes 6 servings*

Prep Time: 15 minutes
Cook Time: 2 hours (LOW) or 1 hour (HIGH)

Sicilian Steak Pinwheels

¾ pound mild or hot Italian sausage, casings removed
1¾ cups fresh bread crumbs
¾ cup grated Parmesan cheese
2 eggs
3 tablespoons minced fresh Italian parsley, plus additional for garnish
1½ to 2 pounds beef round steak
1 cup frozen peas
1 cup pasta sauce
1 cup beef broth

Slow Cooker Directions

1. Lightly coat slow cooker with nonstick cooking spray. Mix sausage, bread crumbs, cheese, eggs and 3 tablespoons parsley in large bowl until well blended; set aside.

2. Place steak between 2 large sheets of plastic wrap. Pound with meat mallet or bottom of skillet until about ⅜ inch thick.

3. Remove top layer of plastic wrap. Spread sausage mixture over steak. Press frozen peas into sausage mixture. Lift edge of plastic wrap at short end to begin rolling steak. Roll up completely; discard plastic wrap. Tie at 2-inch intervals with kitchen twine. Transfer to slow cooker.

4. Combine pasta sauce and broth in medium bowl. Pour over steak. Cover; cook on LOW 6 hours or until tender and cooked through.

5. Transfer steak to serving platter. Let stand 20 minutes, Remove and discard twine; cut steak into 1-inch slices. Skim and discard excess fat from sauce. Serve steak with sauce.

Makes 4 to 6 servings

Prep Time: 20 to 25 minutes
Cook Time: 6 hours

Ham with Fruited Bourbon Sauce

   1 (6-pound) bone-in ham
   ¾ cup packed dark brown sugar
   ½ cup raisins
   ½ cup apple juice
   1 teaspoon ground cinnamon
   ¼ teaspoon red pepper flakes
   ⅓ cup dried cherries
   ¼ cup bourbon, rum or apple juice
   ¼ cup cornstarch

Slow Cooker Directions

1. Lightly coat slow cooker with nonstick cooking spray. Add ham, cut side up. Combine brown sugar, raisins, apple juice, cinnamon and red pepper flakes in small bowl; stir well.

2. Pour mixture evenly over ham. Cover; cook on LOW 9 to 10 hours or on HIGH 4½ to 5 hours. Add cherries 30 minutes before end of cooking time.

3. Transfer ham to cutting board. Let stand 15 minutes before slicing.

4. Meanwhile, pour cooking liquid into large measuring cup and let stand 15 minutes. Skim and discard excess fat. Return cooking liquid to slow cooker.

5. *Turn slow cooker to HIGH.* Stir bourbon into cornstarch in small bowl until smooth. Stir into cooking liquid. Cover; cook on 15 minutes or until thickened. Serve sauce over ham.

Makes 10 to 12 servings

Prep Time: 5 minutes
Cook Time: 9 to 10 hours (LOW) or 4½ to 5 hours (HIGH), plus 30 minutes

Chicken with Artichoke-Parmesan Dressing

2 cans (14 ounces each) quartered artichoke hearts, drained and coarsely chopped

4 ounces herb-seasoned stuffing mix

1½ cups frozen seasoning blend vegetables, thawed*

¾ cup mayonnaise

¾ cup plus 1 tablespoon grated Parmesan cheese, divided

1 egg, beaten

½ teaspoon salt

½ teaspoon paprika

½ teaspoon dried oregano

¼ teaspoon black pepper

6 bone-in chicken breasts (about 3½ pounds)

Seasoning blend is a mixture of chopped bell peppers, onions and celery.

Slow Cooker Directions

1. Lightly coat slow cooker with nonstick cooking spray. Combine artichokes, stuffing mix, vegetables, mayonnaise, ¾ cup Parmesan cheese and egg in large bowl until well blended. Transfer mixture to slow cooker.

2. Combine salt, paprika, oregano and pepper in small bowl. Rub evenly onto chicken. Arrange chicken on top of artichoke mixture, overlapping slightly. Cover; cook on HIGH 3 hours.

3. Transfer chicken to serving platter. Cover with foil to keep warm.

4. Stir artichoke mixture in slow cooker. Sprinkle evenly with remaining 1 tablespoon Parmesan cheese. Cook, uncovered, 20 minutes or until thickened. Serve dressing with chicken.

Makes 6 servings

Prep Time: 5 minutes
Cook Time: 3 hours, plus 20 minutes

Chicken with Artichoke-Parmesan Dressing

Spicy Citrus Turkey Au Jus

   1 bone-in turkey breast (about 4 pounds)
¼ cup (½ stick) butter, softened
    Grated peel of 1 lemon
   1 teaspoon chili powder
¼ to ½ teaspoon black pepper
⅛ to ¼ teaspoon red pepper flakes
   1 tablespoon lemon juice
    Salt and black pepper

Slow Cooker Directions

1. Lightly coat slow cooker with nonstick cooking spray. Add turkey breast.

2. Mix butter, lemon peel, chili powder, black pepper and red pepper flakes in small bowl until well blended. Spread mixture over top and sides of turkey.

3. Cover; cook on LOW 4 to 5 hours or on HIGH 2½ to 3 hours or until meat thermometer reaches 165°F.

4. Transfer turkey to cutting board. Let stand 10 minutes before slicing.

5. Stir lemon juice into cooking liquid. Strain; discard solids. Let mixture stand 15 minutes. Skim and discard excess fat. Season with salt and pepper. Serve sauce with turkey.

Makes 6 to 8 servings

Prep Time: 10 minutes
Cook Time: 4 to 5 hours (LOW) or 2½ to 3 hours (HIGH)

Spicy Citrus Turkey Au Jus

Texas-Style Barbecued Brisket

3 tablespoons Worcestershire sauce
2 cloves garlic, minced
1 tablespoon chili powder
1 teaspoon *each* celery salt, black pepper and liquid smoke
1 beef brisket (3 to 4 pounds), trimmed of fat
2 bay leaves
Barbecue Sauce (recipe follows)

Slow Cooker Directions

1. Combine Worcestershire sauce, garlic, chili powder, celery salt, pepper and liquid smoke in small bowl. Spread mixture on all sides of beef. Place beef in large resealable food storage bag; seal bag. Refrigerate 24 hours.

2. Place beef, marinade and bay leaves in slow cooker, cutting meat in half to fit, if necessary. Cover; cook on LOW 7 hours. Meanwhile, prepare Barbecue Sauce.

3. Remove beef from slow cooker and pour juices into 2-cup measure; let stand 5 minutes. Skim fat from juices. Remove and discard bay leaves. Stir 1 cup juices into Barbecue Sauce. Discard remaining juices.

4. Return beef and barbecue sauce mixture to slow cooker. Cover; cook on LOW 1 hour or until meat is fork-tender. Remove beef to cutting board. Cut across grain into 1/4-inch-thick slices. Serve with sauce. *Makes 10 to 12 servings*

Barbecue Sauce

2 tablespoons vegetable oil
1 onion, chopped
2 cloves garlic, minced
1 cup ketchup
1/2 cup molasses
1/4 cup cider vinegar
2 teaspoons chili powder
1/2 teaspoon dry mustard

Heat oil in medium saucepan over medium heat. Add onion and garlic; cook and stir until onion is tender. Add remaining ingredients. Simmer over medium heat 5 minutes.
Makes about 1 3/4 cups sauce

Best Ever Barbecued Ribs

1 teaspoon salt
1 teaspoon dried thyme
1 teaspoon paprika
¼ teaspoon black pepper
⅛ teaspoon ground red pepper
3 to 3½ pounds well trimmed pork baby back ribs, cut into 4-rib pieces
¼ cup ketchup
2 tablespoons brown sugar
1 tablespoon Worcestershire sauce
1 tablespoon soy sauce

Slow Cooker Directions

1. Lightly coat slow cooker with nonstick cooking spray. Combine salt, thyme, paprika, black pepper and red pepper in small bowl; rub onto meaty side of ribs. Place ribs in slow cooker.

2. Cover; cook on LOW 7 to 8 hours or on HIGH 3 to 4 hours. Remove ribs from slow cooker; discard liquid.

3. Combine ketchup, brown sugar, Worcestershire sauce and soy sauce in medium bowl until well blended.

4. *Turn slow cooker to HIGH.* Coat ribs with sauce mixture; return to slow cooker. Cook 30 minutes or until ribs are glazed. *Makes 6 servings*

Prep Time: 5 minutes
Cook Time: 7 to 8 hours (LOW) or 3 to 4 hours (HIGH), plus 30 minutes

✳**Tip** Worcestershire sauce is a dark, savory sauce developed in India and named after the English town, Worcester, where it was first bottled. Made from a complex and seemingly incompatible mix of ingredients, including anchovies, tamarind paste, molasses, onions, garlic and soy sauce, it is used as a seasoning in sauces, gravies and soups.

Special Sauerbraten

2 cups water
2 cups dry red wine
2 cups red wine vinegar
2 onions, sliced
2 carrots, sliced
¼ cup plus 2 tablespoons sugar, divided
1 tablespoon dried parsley flakes
3 teaspoons salt, divided
1 teaspoon mustard seeds
6 peppercorns
6 whole cloves
4 juniper berries*
4 bay leaves
1 beef round tip roast (about 5 pounds)
4 tablespoons all-purpose flour, divided
¼ teaspoon black pepper
2 tablespoons oil
⅓ cup gingersnap crumbs

*Juniper berries are available in the spice aisle at large supermarkets or from mail order spice purveyors.

Slow Cooker Directions

1. Stir together water, wine, vinegar, onions, carrots, ¼ cup sugar, parsley flakes, 2 teaspoons salt, mustard seeds, peppercorns, cloves, juniper berries and bay leaves in medium saucepan. Bring to a boil over medium-high heat. Reduce heat to medium-low; simmer 15 minutes. Cool completely. Place roast in large glass bowl or large resealable food storage bag; pour mixture over roast. Cover or seal bag. Marinate in refrigerator up to 2 days, turning once a day.

2. Remove roast from marinade. Strain marinade; discard solids. Dry meat with paper towel. Stir together 2 tablespoons flour, remaining 1 teaspoon salt and pepper in small bowl; spread on all sides of roast. Heat oil in large skillet over medium heat; brown roast on all sides.

3. Transfer roast to slow cooker; add 1½ cups strained marinade. Discard remaining marinade. Cover; cook on LOW 8 hours.

4. *Turn slow cooker to HIGH.* Combine remaining 2 tablespoons sugar, 2 tablespoons flour and gingersnap crumbs in small bowl; stir into slow cooker. Cover; cook 30 minutes or until juices are thickened. Remove roast from slow cooker; let stand 15 minutes. Slice roast and serve with juices.

Makes 6 to 8 servings

TABLE OF CONTENTS

Carrot Soup

  2 teaspoons butter
 ¹⁄₃ cup chopped onion
  1 tablespoon chopped fresh ginger
  1 pound baby carrots
 ¹⁄₂ teaspoon salt
 ¹⁄₄ teaspoon black pepper
  3 cups vegetable broth
 ¹⁄₄ cup whipping cream
 ¹⁄₄ cup orange juice
  Pinch ground nutmeg
  4 tablespoons sour cream

1. Melt butter in large saucepan over medium-high heat. Add onion and ginger; cook and stir 1 minute or until ginger is fragrant. Add carrots, salt and pepper; cook and stir 2 minutes.

2. Stir in broth; bring to a boil. Reduce heat to medium-low; cover and simmer 30 minutes or until carrots are tender.

3. Working in batches, process soup in blender or food processor until smooth. Return to saucepan; stir in cream, orange juice and nutmeg. Cook over medium heat until heated through, stirring occasionally. Thin soup with additional broth, if necessary. Top soup with sour cream just before serving. *Makes 4 servings*

Summer's Best Gazpacho

      3 cups tomato juice
   2½ cups finely diced tomatoes
      1 cup finely diced yellow or red bell pepper
      1 cup finely diced unpeeled cucumber
      ½ cup chunky salsa
      1 tablespoon olive oil
      1 clove garlic, minced
      1 ripe avocado, diced
      ¼ cup finely chopped fresh cilantro or basil

1. Combine tomato juice, tomatoes, bell pepper, cucumber, salsa, oil and garlic in large bowl; mix well. Cover and chill at least 1 hour or up to 24 hours before serving.

2. Stir in avocado and cilantro just before serving.   *Makes 4 to 6 servings*

Broccoli Cream Soup with Green Onions

      1 tablespoon olive oil
      2 cups chopped onions
      1 pound fresh or frozen broccoli florets or spears
      2 cups vegetable or chicken broth
      6 tablespoons cream cheese
      1 cup milk
      ¾ teaspoon salt
      ⅛ teaspoon ground red pepper
      ⅓ cup finely chopped green onions

1. Heat oil in large saucepan over medium-high heat. Add onions; cook and stir 4 minutes or until translucent. Add broccoli and broth; bring to a boil. Reduce heat to medium-low; cover and simmer 10 minutes or until broccoli is tender.

2. Working in batches, process soup in food processor or blender until smooth. Return to saucepan; heat over medium heat.

3. Whisk in cream cheese until melted. Stir in milk, salt and red pepper; cook 2 minutes or until heated through. Top with green onions.   *Makes 4 to 6 servings*

Madeira Mushroom and Leek Soup

  6 cups SWANSON® Vegetable Broth (Regular or Certified Organic)
½ cup Madeira wine
  1 ounce dried shiitake, morel or cepes mushrooms
  4 tablespoons butter
  3 leeks, white part only, coarsely chopped (about 2 cups)
  2 tablespoons all-purpose flour
  1 package (8 ounces) sliced white mushrooms (about 3 cups)
¼ teaspoon ground black pepper
    Additional chopped mushrooms and chopped leeks

1. Heat **1 cup** broth, wine and dried mushrooms in a 1-quart saucepan over high heat to a boil. Remove the saucepan from the heat. Let stand for 30 minutes. Do not drain.

2. Heat the butter in a 4-quart saucepan over low heat. Add the leeks and cook until they're tender-crisp. Stir in the flour. Cook and stir for 5 minutes.

3. Gradually stir in the remaining broth, fresh mushrooms, black pepper and the dried mushroom mixture. Heat to a boil. Reduce the heat to low. Cook for 30 minutes or until the mushrooms are tender.

4. Place ⅓ of the mushroom mixture into a blender or food processor. Cover and blend until the mixture is smooth. Pour the mixture into a large bowl. Repeat twice more with the remaining mushroom mixture. Return all the puréed mixture to the saucepan. Cook over medium heat for 5 minutes or until the mixture is hot and bubbling.

5. Divide the soup among **6** serving bowls. Garnish with the additional mushrooms and leeks.

Makes 6 servings

Tip Madeira is a golden-colored wine that can be used for drinking as well as cooking. American-made Madeiras are often much more reasonably priced than those produced in Portugal.

Hearty Vegetable Stew

1 tablespoon olive oil
1 cup chopped onion
¾ cup chopped carrots
3 cloves garlic, minced
4 cups coarsely chopped green cabbage
3½ cups coarsely chopped unpeeled new red potatoes
1 teaspoon salt
1 teaspoon dried rosemary
½ teaspoon black pepper
4 cups vegetable broth
1 can (15 ounces) Great Northern beans, rinsed and drained
1 can (about 14 ounces) diced tomatoes
Grated Parmesan cheese (optional)

1. Heat oil in large saucepan over medium-high heat. Add onion and carrots; cook and stir 3 minutes. Add garlic; cook and stir 1 minute.

2. Add cabbage, potatoes, salt, rosemary and pepper; cook 1 minute. Stir in broth, beans and tomatoes; bring to a boil. Reduce heat to medium-low; simmer 15 minutes or until potatoes are tender. Sprinkle with cheese, if desired.   *Makes 6 to 8 servings*

Sweet Potato Bisque with Ginger

2 cans (15 ounces each) sweet potatoes in heavy syrup, drained
1 can (about 13 ounces) coconut milk
1 cup vegetable or chicken broth
1 green onion, cut into thirds
¼ teaspoon salt
⅛ teaspoon ground red pepper
2 teaspoons grated fresh ginger or crystallized ginger

1. Combine sweet potatoes, coconut milk, broth, green onion, salt and red pepper in food processor or blender; process until smooth.

2. Transfer to large saucepan. Bring to a boil, stirring frequently. Reduce heat to medium-low; simmer 3 minutes. Remove from heat; stir in ginger.   *Makes 2 to 4 servings*

Cream of Pumpkin Soup with Cranberry Drizzle

3½ cups SWANSON® Vegetable Broth (Regular or Certified Organic)

1 tablespoon olive oil

1 tablespoon packed brown sugar

1 cup whole cranberry sauce

2 tablespoons butter

1 large onion, chopped (about 1 cup)

¼ teaspoon ground cinnamon

⅛ teaspoon ground ginger

Freshly ground black pepper

1 pumpkin or calabaza squash (about 2½ pounds), peeled, seeded and cut into 1-inch pieces (5 to 6 cups)

2 tablespoons light cream (optional)

1. Stir ¼ **cup** broth, oil, brown sugar and cranberry sauce in a small bowl.

2. Heat the butter in a 4-quart saucepan over medium heat. Add the onion and cook until it's tender.

3. Add the remaining broth, cinnamon, ginger, black pepper to taste and pumpkin to the saucepan. Heat to a boil. Reduce the heat to low. Cover and cook for 10 minutes or until the pumpkin is tender.

4. Place **half** the pumpkin mixture into a blender or food processor. Cover and blend until the mixture is smooth. Pour the mixture into a large bowl. Repeat with the remaining pumpkin mixture. Return the puréed mixture to the saucepan. Add the cream, if desired. Cook until the mixture is hot and bubbling. Divide the soup among **8** serving bowls. Top **each** with a spoonful of the cranberry sauce mixture. *Makes 8 servings*

Prep Time: 20 minutes
Cook Time: 20 minutes

Greens, White Bean and Barley Soup

2 tablespoons olive oil

3 carrots, diced

1½ cups chopped onions

2 cloves garlic, minced

1½ cups sliced mushrooms

6 cups vegetable broth

2 cups cooked barley

1 can (about 15 ounces) Great Northern beans, rinsed and drained

2 bay leaves

1 teaspoon sugar

1 teaspoon dried thyme

7 cups chopped stemmed collard greens (about 24 ounces)

1 tablespoon white wine vinegar

Hot pepper sauce

Red bell pepper strips (optional)

1. Heat oil in Dutch oven over medium heat. Add carrots, onions and garlic; cook and stir 3 minutes. Add mushrooms; cook and stir 5 minutes or until carrots are tender.

2. Add broth, barley, beans, bay leaves, sugar and thyme. Bring to a boil over high heat. Reduce heat to medium-low; cover and simmer 5 minutes. Add greens; simmer 10 minutes. Remove and discard bay leaves. Stir in vinegar. Season with hot pepper sauce. Garnish with red bell pepper.   *Makes 6 to 8 servings*

Tip Collard greens have tough stems that should be removed before cooking. To remove the stems, fold each leaf in half. With your fingers, pull the stem toward the top of the leaf. Discard the stems.

Celery-Leek Bisque with Basil

3 bunches leeks (3 pounds), trimmed and well rinsed*
2 stalks celery, sliced
1 carrot, peeled and sliced
3 cloves garlic, minced
2 cans (about 14 ounces each) vegetable or chicken broth
1 package (8 ounces) cream cheese with garlic and herbs
2 cups half-and-half, plus additional for garnish
    Salt and black pepper
    Fresh basil leaves

*Thoroughly rinsing the leeks is very important. Gritty sand can get between the layers of the leeks and can be difficult to see, so you may need to rinse them several times.

Slow Cooker Directions

1. Chop leeks; place in slow cooker. Add celery, carrot and garlic; pour in broth. Cover; cook on LOW 8 hours or on HIGH 4 hours.

2. Working in batches, process soup in blender or food processor until smooth. Add cream cheese to last batch. Return to slow cooker. Stir in 2 cups half-and-half. Season with salt and pepper. For best flavor, cool to room temperature and refrigerate overnight. Reheat in large saucepan over medium heat before serving. Garnish with swirl of half-and-half and basil.

Makes 4 to 6 servings

Prep Time: 45 minutes
Cook Time: 8 hours (LOW) or 4 hours (HIGH)

Easy Salsa Soup

2 jars (16 ounces each) ORTEGA® Original Salsa
1 package (8 ounces) cream cheese
4 ORTEGA® Taco Shells, crumbled

Combine salsa and cream cheese in large saucepan. Cook and stir over medium heat 5 minutes or until cream cheese melts. Reduce heat to medium-low and cook 5 minutes longer.

Pour into blender or food processor in two batches. Pulse several times until well combined. Pour back into saucepan; cook over low heat 5 minutes longer. Serve with crumbled shells.

Makes 6 servings

Celery-Leek Bisque with Basil

Curried Vegetable-Rice Soup

        1 package (16 ounces) frozen stir-fry vegetables
        1 can (about 14 ounces) vegetable broth
    $3/4$ cup uncooked instant brown rice
        2 teaspoons curry powder
    $1/2$ teaspoon salt
    $1/2$ teaspoon hot pepper sauce
        1 can (14 ounces) unsweetened coconut milk
        1 tablespoon lime juice

1. Combine vegetables and broth in large saucepan. Cover; bring to a boil over high heat. Stir in rice, curry powder, salt and hot pepper sauce. Reduce heat to medium-low; cover and simmer 8 minutes or until rice is tender, stirring once.

2. Stir in coconut milk; cook 3 minutes or until heated through. Remove from heat; stir in lime juice. Serve immediately. *Makes 4 servings*

Cream of Asparagus Soup

        1 pound asparagus
    $3^1/2$ cups vegetable or chicken broth, divided
    $1/4$ cup ($1/2$ stick) butter
    $1/4$ cup all-purpose flour
    $1/2$ cup whipping cream
    $1/2$ teaspoon salt
    $1/8$ teaspoon black pepper

1. Trim off and discard tough ends of asparagus. Cut asparagus into 1-inch pieces. Combine asparagus and 1 cup broth in medium saucepan; cook 12 to 15 minutes or until tender.

2. Remove 1 cup asparagus pieces; reserve. Process remaining asparagus pieces with broth in blender or food processor until smooth.

3. Melt butter in large saucepan. Stir in flour until smooth. Gradually add remaining $2^1/2$ cups broth; cook until slightly thickened, stirring occasionally. Stir in cream, salt, pepper, asparagus mixture and reserved asparagus pieces; cook until heated through. *Makes 6 to 8 servings*

Corn and Buttermilk Blender Chowder

    3 cups buttermilk, divided
    2 cups corn
    3 green onions, coarsely chopped
 1½ tablespoons coarsely chopped fresh cilantro, plus additional for garnish
    ¼ teaspoon salt
    ⅛ teaspoon black pepper

1. Combine 1 cup buttermilk, corn, green onions, cilantro, salt and pepper in blender. Process using on/off pulsing action until corn and green onions are finely chopped. Pour mixture into pitcher; stir in remaining 2 cups buttermilk.

2. Serve immediately or refrigerate up to 4 hours. Stir well before serving. Garnish with additional cilantro, if desired. *Makes 4 servings*

Vegetable Minestrone Soup

    2 tablespoons olive or vegetable oil
    2 medium zucchini, cut in half lengthwise and thickly sliced (about 3 cups)
    2 cloves garlic, minced
  ½ teaspoon dried rosemary leaves, crushed
    4 cups SWANSON® Vegetable Broth (Regular or Certified Organic)
    1 can (about 14½ ounces) diced tomatoes, drained
    1 can (about 19 ounces) white kidney beans (cannellini), rinsed and drained
  ½ cup uncooked corkscrew-shaped pasta (rotini)
  ¼ cup grated Parmesan cheese (optional)

1. Heat the oil in a 6-quart saucepot. Add the zucchini, garlic and rosemary and cook until the zucchini is tender-crisp.

2. Stir the broth and tomatoes into the saucepot and heat to a boil. Reduce the heat to low. Cover and cook for 10 minutes.

3. Increase the heat to medium. Stir in the beans and pasta. Cook for 10 minutes or until the pasta is tender. Serve with the cheese, if desired. *Makes 8 servings*

Prep Time: 10 minutes
Cook Time: 30 minutes

SOUP FOR SUPPER

Black Bean and Bacon Soup

   5 strips bacon, sliced
   1 medium onion, diced
   2 tablespoons ORTEGA® Diced Green Chiles
   2 cans (15 ounces each) JOAN OF ARC® Black Beans, undrained
   4 cups chicken broth
½ cup ORTEGA® Taco Sauce
½ cup sour cream
   4 ORTEGA® Yellow Corn Taco Shells, crumbled

Cook bacon in large pot over medium heat 5 minutes or until crisp. Add onion and chiles. Cook 5 minutes or until onion begins to brown. Stir in beans, broth and taco sauce. Bring to a boil. Reduce heat to low. Simmer 20 minutes.

Purée half of soup in food processor until smooth (or use immersion blender in pot). Return puréed soup to pot and stir to combine. Serve with a dollop of sour cream and crumbled taco shells. *Makes 6 to 8 servings*

Note: For a less chunky soup, purée the entire batch and cook an additional 15 minutes.

Prep Time: 5 minutes
Start to Finish: 30 minutes

Chile Verde Chicken Stew

$1/3$ cup all-purpose flour
$1^1/2$ teaspoons salt, divided
$1/4$ teaspoon black pepper
$1^1/2$ pounds boneless skinless chicken breasts, cut into $1^1/2$-inch pieces
4 tablespoons vegetable oil, divided
1 pound tomatillos (about 9), husked and halved
2 onions, chopped
2 cans (4 ounces each) mild green chiles
1 tablespoon dried oregano
1 tablespoon ground cumin
2 cloves garlic, chopped
1 teaspoon sugar
2 cups chicken broth
8 ounces Mexican lager
5 unpeeled red potatoes, diced
Chopped fresh cilantro, sour cream, shredded Monterey Jack cheese, lime wedges, diced avocado and/or hot pepper sauce (optional)

1. Combine flour, 1 teaspoon salt and pepper in large bowl. Add chicken; toss to coat. Heat 2 tablespoons oil in large nonstick skillet over medium heat. Add chicken; cook until lightly browned on all sides, stirring occasionally. Transfer to Dutch oven.

2. Heat remaining 2 tablespoons oil in same skillet. Stir in tomatillos, onions, chiles, oregano, cumin, garlic, sugar and remaining $1/2$ teaspoon salt. Cook and stir 20 minutes or until vegetables are softened. Stir in broth and lager.

3. Working in batches, process soup in food processor or blender until almost smooth. Transfer to Dutch oven. Stir in potatoes. Cover; bring to a boil over medium-high heat. Reduce heat to low; simmer, covered, 1 hour or until potatoes are tender, stirring occasionally. Serve in shallow bowls with desired toppings.   *Makes 6 servings*

Sausage and Bean Ragoût

2 tablespoons olive oil

1 pound ground beef

1 pound hot Italian pork sausage, casing removed

1 large onion, chopped (about 1 cup)

4 cloves garlic, minced

3½ cups SWANSON® Chicken Stock

¼ cup chopped fresh basil leaves

2 cans (about 14½ ounces each) diced tomatoes with Italian herbs

1 can (about 15 ounces) white kidney beans (cannellini), rinsed and drained

½ cup uncooked elbow pasta

1 bag (6 ounces) fresh baby spinach leaves

⅓ cup grated Romano cheese

1. Heat the oil in a 6-quart saucepot over medium-high heat. Add the beef, sausage and onion and cook until the beef and sausage are well browned, stirring often to separate meat. Pour off any fat. Add the garlic and cook for 30 seconds.

2. Stir the stock, basil, tomatoes and beans in the saucepot and heat to a boil. Reduce the heat to low. Cover and cook for 10 minutes, stirring occasionally. Add the pasta and cook until it's tender.

3. Stir in the spinach and cook until the spinach is wilted. Remove the saucepot from the heat and stir in the cheese. Serve with additional cheese, if desired.   *Makes 6 servings*

Kitchen Tip: In Step 2, the recipe calls for cooking the pasta until it's tender. However, if you like your pasta a little al dente, that will work as well.

Prep Time: 15 minutes
Cook Time: 40 minutes

Turkey Split Pea Soup

    7 cups low-sodium chicken broth
    1 pound dried split peas, washed and drained
    2 cups chopped onions
    1 cup chopped carrots
 $\frac{1}{2}$ cup chopped celery
    1 clove garlic, minced
    3 tablespoons dried parsley
    1 bay leaf
    1 pound turkey ham, cut into $\frac{1}{2}$-inch cubes

In 5-quart saucepan, over high heat, combine broth, peas, onions, carrots, celery, garlic, parsley and bay leaf; bring to a boil. Reduce heat to simmer, cover and cook 1 hour. Remove saucepan from heat and discard bay leaf.

With wire whisk, gently whisk soup to blend peas. If desired, soup can be processed in food processor or blender for smoother texture.

Return soup to medium-high heat, add turkey ham and bring to a boil. Reduce heat to simmer and cook, uncovered, 10 to 15 minutes. *Makes 8 servings*

Favorite recipe from *National Turkey Federation*

Zesty Chicken & Vegetable Soup

 $\frac{1}{2}$ pound boneless skinless chicken breasts, cut into very thin strips
    1 to 2 tablespoons *Frank's® RedHot®* Original Cayenne Pepper Sauce
    4 cups chicken broth
    1 package (16 ounces) frozen stir-fry vegetables
    1 cup angel hair pasta or fine egg noodles, broken into 2-inch lengths
    1 green onion, thinly sliced

1. Combine chicken and *Frank's RedHot* Sauce in medium bowl; set aside.

2. Heat broth to boiling in large saucepan over medium-high heat. Add vegetables and pasta; return to boiling. Cook 2 minutes. Stir in chicken mixture and green onion. Cook 1 minute or until chicken is no longer pink. *Makes 4 to 6 servings*

Italian-Style Meatball Soup

½ pound ground beef
¼ pound bulk Italian sausage
 1 onion, finely chopped, divided
⅓ cup plain dry bread crumbs
 1 egg
½ teaspoon salt
 4 cups beef broth
 2 cups water
 1 can (8 ounces) stewed tomatoes
 1 can (8 ounces) pizza sauce
 2 cups sliced cabbage
 1 can (about 15 ounces) kidney beans, rinsed and drained
 2 carrots, sliced
½ cup frozen Italian green beans

1. Combine beef, sausage, 2 tablespoons onion, bread crumbs, egg and salt in large bowl; mix until well blended. Shape into 32 (1-inch) meatballs.

2. Brown half of meatballs in large skillet over medium heat, turning frequently. Remove from skillet; drain on paper towels. Repeat with remaining meatballs.

3. Bring broth, water, tomatoes and pizza sauce to a boil in Dutch oven over medium-high heat. Add meatballs, remaining onion, cabbage, beans and carrots; bring to a boil. Reduce heat to medium-low; simmer 20 minutes. Add green beans; simmer 10 minutes.

Makes 8 servings

Turkey Taco Soup

> 1 tablespoon olive oil
> $\frac{1}{2}$ cup diced onions
> 1 tablespoon POLANER® Minced Garlic
> 1 pound ground turkey
> 1 tablespoon ORTEGA® Chili Seasoning Mix
> $\frac{1}{2}$ teaspoon salt
> $\frac{1}{2}$ teaspoon black pepper
> 3 cups chicken broth
> 1 can (16 ounces) ORTEGA® Refried Beans
> 1 tablespoon ORTEGA® Fire-Roasted Chiles
> 1 cup shredded lettuce
> $\frac{1}{2}$ cup chopped tomato
> 4 ORTEGA® Taco Shells, broken into small pieces

Heat olive oil in large saucepan over medium heat. Add onions and garlic; cook and stir 5 minutes. Stir in turkey, seasoning mix, salt and pepper. Cook and stir 5 minutes to break up turkey.

Add broth, beans and chiles; stir until beans are mixed in well. Cook over medium heat 10 minutes.

Divide soup among 6 bowls. Divide lettuce among bowls, and stir in to wilt lettuce slightly. Top each serving with chopped tomatoes and taco pieces.   *Makes 6 servings*

Prep Time: 5 minutes
Start-to-Finish Time: 30 minutes

Beefy Broccoli & Cheese Soup

        2 cups beef broth
        1 package (10 ounces) frozen chopped broccoli, thawed
    ¼ cup chopped onion
    ¼ pound ground beef
        1 cup milk
        2 tablespoons all-purpose flour
        1 cup (4 ounces) shredded sharp Cheddar cheese
    1½ teaspoons chopped fresh oregano *or* ½ teaspoon dried oregano
            Salt and black pepper
            Hot pepper sauce

1. Bring broth to a boil in medium saucepan over high heat. Add broccoli and onion; cook 5 minutes or until broccoli is tender.

2. Brown beef in large nonstick skillet over medium-high heat 6 to 8 minutes, stirring to break up meat. Drain fat. Stir milk into flour in small bowl until smooth.

3. Add milk mixture and beef to broth mixture; cook and stir until mixture is thickened and heated through.

4. Add cheese and oregano; stir until cheese is melted. Season with salt, black pepper and hot pepper sauce.   *Makes 4 servings*

Kansas City Beef Soup

    ½ pound ground beef
        3 cups frozen mixed vegetables
        2 cups water
        1 can (about 14 ounces) stewed tomatoes
        1 cup chopped onion
        1 cup sliced celery
        1 beef bouillon cube
    ½ to 1 teaspoon black pepper
        1 can (about 14 ounces) beef broth
    ½ cup all-purpose flour

1. Brown beef in large saucepan over medium-high heat 6 to 8 minutes, stirring to break up meat. Drain fat.

continued on page 194

Kansas City Beef Soup, continued

2. Add mixed vegetables, water, tomatoes, onion, celery, bouillon and pepper to saucepan; bring to a boil.

3. Stir broth into flour in small bowl until smooth. Add to beef mixture; stir until blended. Bring to a boil. Reduce heat to medium-low; cover and simmer 15 minutes, stirring frequently.

Makes 6 servings

Chicken and Wild Rice Soup

> 5 cups chicken broth, divided
> $\frac{1}{2}$ cup uncooked wild rice, rinsed and drained
> $\frac{1}{4}$ cup ($\frac{1}{2}$ stick) butter
> 1 carrot, sliced
> 1 onion, chopped
> 2 stalks celery, chopped
> $\frac{1}{2}$ (8-ounce) package mushrooms, sliced
> 2 tablespoons all-purpose flour
> $\frac{1}{4}$ teaspoon salt
> $\frac{1}{4}$ teaspoon white pepper
> 1$\frac{1}{2}$ cups chopped cooked chicken
> $\frac{1}{4}$ cup dry sherry (optional)

1. Combine 2$\frac{1}{2}$ cups broth and rice in medium saucepan; bring to a boil. Reduce heat to medium-low; cover and simmer 1 hour or until rice is tender. Drain; set aside.

2. Melt butter in large saucepan over medium heat. Add carrot; cook and stir 3 minutes. Add onion, celery and mushrooms; cook and stir 3 to 4 minutes or until tender. Whisk in flour, salt and white pepper until smooth.

3. Gradually stir in remaining 2$\frac{1}{2}$ cups broth. Bring to a boil. Reduce heat to medium-low; cook and stir 2 minutes or until thickened. Stir in chicken, rice and sherry, if desired. Simmer 3 minutes or until heated through.

Makes 4 to 6 servings

Smoky Navy Bean Soup

        2 tablespoons olive oil, divided
        4 ounces ham or Canadian bacon, diced
        1 cup diced onion
        1 carrot, thinly sliced
        1 stalk celery, thinly sliced
        3 cups water
        6 ounces unpeeled red potatoes, diced
        2 bay leaves
      ¼ teaspoon dried tarragon
        1 can (about 15 ounces) navy beans, rinsed and drained
      1½ teaspoons liquid smoke
        Salt and black pepper

1. Heat 1 tablespoon oil in large saucepan over medium-high heat. Add ham; cook and stir 2 minutes or until browned. Remove to paper towel-lined plate.

2. Add onion, carrot and celery to same saucepan; cook and stir 4 minutes or until onion is translucent. Add water; bring to a boil. Add potatoes, bay leaves and tarragon. Reduce heat to medium-low; cover and simmer 20 minutes or until potatoes are tender. Remove from heat.

3. Stir in beans, ham, remaining 1 tablespoon oil and liquid smoke. Remove and discard bay leaves. Season with salt and pepper.

Makes 6 servings

Roasted Corn and Chicken Soup

   4 tablespoons olive oil, divided
   1 can (15 ounces) yellow corn, drained
   1 can (15 ounces) white corn, drained
   1 onion, diced
   3 tablespoons ORTEGA® Diced Green Chiles
   ½ of (1½- to 2-pound) cooked rotisserie chicken, bones removed and meat shredded
   1 packet (1.25 ounces) ORTEGA® Taco Seasoning Mix
   4 cups chicken broth
   4 ORTEGA® Yellow Corn Taco Shells, crumbled

Heat 2 tablespoons olive oil in large skillet over medium heat until hot. Add corn. Cook until brown, about 8 minutes; stir often to prevent corn from burning. Add remaining 2 tablespoons olive oil, onion and chiles. Cook and stir 3 minutes longer.

Transfer mixture to large pot. Stir in shredded chicken. Add seasoning mix and toss to combine. Stir in chicken broth and bring to a boil. Reduce heat to low. Simmer 15 minutes. Serve with crumbled taco shells.   *Makes 8 servings*

Prep Time: 15 minutes
Start-to-Finish Time: 30 minutes

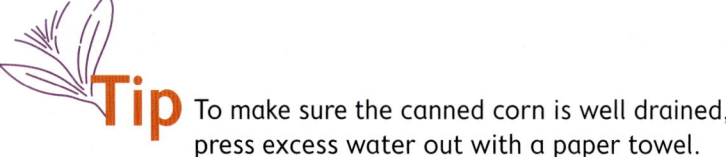

Tip To make sure the canned corn is well drained, press excess water out with a paper towel.

Lamb Meatball & Bean Soup

        1 pound ground lamb
      ¼ cup chopped onion
        1 clove garlic, minced
        1 teaspoon ground cumin
      ½ teaspoon salt
        2 cups chicken broth
        1 package (10 ounces) frozen chopped broccoli *or* 1½ cups fresh broccoli florets
        1 tomato, peeled and chopped
        1 can (about 15 ounces) chickpeas or black-eyed peas, rinsed and drained
      ½ teaspoon dried thyme
          Salt and black pepper

1. Combine lamb, onion, garlic, cumin and salt in medium bowl; mix lightly. Shape into 1-inch balls.* Brown meatballs in large skillet over medium-high heat, turning occasionally.

2. Meanwhile, bring broth to a boil in large saucepan over high heat. Add broccoli and tomato; bring to a boil.

3. Reduce heat to medium-low. Add meatballs, chickpeas and thyme; cover and simmer 5 minutes or until heated through. Season with salt and pepper.   *Makes 4 to 6 servings*

To quickly shape uniform meatballs, place lamb mixture on cutting board; pat evenly into large square about 1 inch thick. Cut into 1-inch squares; shape each square into a ball.

Ground Beef, Spinach and Barley Soup

　　1 pound ground beef
　　4 cups water
　　1 can (about 14 ounces) stewed tomatoes
1½ cups thinly sliced carrots
　　1 cup chopped onion
　½ cup quick-cooking barley
1½ teaspoons beef bouillon granules
1½ teaspoons dried thyme
　　1 teaspoon dried oregano
　½ teaspoon garlic powder
　¼ teaspoon black pepper
　⅛ teaspoon salt
　　3 cups torn stemmed spinach leaves

1. Brown beef in large saucepan over medium-high heat 6 to 8 minutes, stirring to break up meat. Drain fat.

2. Stir in water, tomatoes, carrots, onion, barley, bouillon, thyme, oregano, garlic powder, pepper and salt. Bring to a boil over high heat.

3. Reduce heat to medium-low; cover and simmer 12 to 15 minutes or until barley and vegetables are tender, stirring occasionally.

4. Stir in spinach; cook until wilted, stirring occasionally. Serve immediately.

Makes 6 servings

Corn and Crab Gazpacho

1 cucumber, peeled, seeded and coarsely chopped

3 green onions, coarsely chopped

2 tablespoons coarsely chopped fresh Italian parsley or cilantro

2 pounds grape or cherry tomatoes

1 cup cooked fresh corn (1 large ear) *or* 1 cup thawed frozen corn

3 cups tomato juice, chilled

3 tablespoons olive oil

2 tablespoons red wine vinegar

1¼ teaspoons red pepper flakes

1 teaspoon salt

¼ teaspoon black pepper

1½ cups flaked cooked crabmeat (about 8 ounces) *or* 8 ounces cooked baby shrimp

1. Combine cucumber, green onions and parsley in food processor. Process using on/off pulsing action until finely chopped. Transfer to large pitcher or bowl. Add tomatoes to food processor. Process using on/off pulsing action until finely chopped. Add to cucumber mixture.

2. Stir corn into pitcher. Add tomato juice, oil, vinegar, red pepper flakes, salt and black pepper. Stir well. Cover; refrigerate 1 to 3 hours.

3. Pour gazpacho into 6 bowls. Top each serving with ¼ cup crabmeat.   *Makes 6 servings*

Cajun Shrimp and Potato Chowder

    1 tablespoon olive oil
    ½ pound medium shrimp (26 to 30 count), peeled, deveined (thawed if frozen)
    ½ cup chopped onion
    ½ cup chopped green bell pepper
    2 cups SIMPLY POTATOES® Homestyle Slices, chopped slightly
    1 can (14 ounces) chicken broth
    2 teaspoons Cajun seasoning
    2 tablespoons all-purpose flour
    2 tablespoons water
    1 can (14.5 ounces) diced tomatoes, undrained

1. Heat oil in 2-quart saucepan over medium heat. Add shrimp, onion and green pepper. Cook, stirring occasionally, until shrimp is no longer pink. Add **Simply Potatoes®**, broth and Cajun seasoning. Bring to a boil. Reduce heat to low. Cook, stirring occasionally, until **Simply Potatoes®** are tender (20 to 25 minutes).

2. In small bowl, combine flour and water; stir until smooth. Add flour mixture to soup. Stir in tomatoes. Cook until mixture is thickened and heated through.   *Makes 4 servings*

Oyster Stew

    1 quart shucked oysters, with their liquor
    8 cups milk
    8 tablespoons margarine, cut into pieces
    1 teaspoon freshly ground white pepper
    ½ teaspoon salt
        Paprika
    2 tablespoons finely chopped fresh parsley

Heat oysters in their liquor in medium saucepan over high heat until oyster edges begin to curl, about 2 to 3 minutes. Heat milk and margarine together in large saucepan over medium-high heat just to boiling. Add pepper and salt.

Stir in oysters and their liquor. Do not boil or overcook stew or oysters may get tough. Pour stew into tureen. Dust with paprika; sprinkle with parsley.   *Makes 8 servings*

Favorite recipe from **National Fisheries Institute**

California Fish Stew

    1 quart mussels (in shells), cleaned*
    3 cups Zinfandel or other dry red wine, divided
 ½ cup olive oil
    1 package (8 ounces) mushrooms, sliced
    1 green bell pepper, chopped
    1 onion, chopped
    2 cloves garlic, minced
    1 can (about 28 ounces) whole Italian plum tomatoes, undrained
 ¼ cup tomato paste
    1 teaspoon salt
 ½ teaspoon black pepper
    3 pounds striped bass or other firm fish fillets, cut into bite-size pieces
    2 tablespoons finely chopped fresh basil
    1 pound crabmeat, picked over to remove any shell
    1 pound medium raw shrimp, peeled
    3 tablespoons chopped fresh Italian parsley

*Discard mussels that stay open when tapped with your fingers. To clean mussels, scrub with stiff brush under cold running water. To debeard, pull threads from shells with fingers.

1. Bring 1 cup wine to a boil in large Dutch oven. Add mussels; cover and reduce heat to low. Steam 5 to 7 minutes or until shells open. Transfer to large bowl with slotted spoon. (Discard any unopened shells.) Strain cooking liquid through cheesecloth; set aside.

2. Heat oil in same Dutch oven. Add mushrooms, bell pepper, onion and garlic; cook and stir 3 minutes. Add tomatoes; cook 4 minutes. Stir in reserved cooking liquid, tomato paste and remaining 2 cups wine. Add salt and pepper; simmer 20 minutes.

3. Add fish and basil; cook 2 minutes. Add mussels, crabmeat and shrimp. Cook 3 minutes or until shrimp turn pink and opaque, stirring occasionally. Sprinkle with parsley; serve immediately. *Makes 10 to 12 servings*

New England Clam Chowder

Nonstick cooking spray
4 ounces smoked sausage, finely chopped
1½ cups chopped onions
2¾ cups milk
2 red potatoes, diced
1 can (6½ ounces) minced clams, drained, liquid reserved
2 bay leaves
½ teaspoon dried thyme
2 tablespoons butter
¼ teaspoon black pepper
15 saltine crackers

1. Spray Dutch oven with cooking spray; heat over medium-high heat. Add sausage; cook and stir 2 minutes or until browned. Transfer to plate.

2. Add onions; cook and stir 2 minutes. Add milk, potatoes, reserved clam liquid, bay leaves and thyme. Reduce heat to low; cover and simmer 15 minutes or until potatoes are tender.

3. Remove bay leaves. Stir in sausage, clams, butter and pepper. Simmer until heated through, stirring frequently. Crumble crackers over chowder just before serving.   *Makes 4 servings*

Potato and Salmon Bisque

1 (7½-ounce) can salmon, drained and flaked
1 (14½-ounce) can chicken broth, undiluted
1½ cups skim milk
3 green onions, chopped
2 tablespoons chopped green or red bell pepper
1 teaspoon grated lemon rind or 1 tablespoon lemon juice
⅛ teaspoon black pepper
½ cup IDAHO® instant mashed potato granules

Microwave Directions

Combine salmon, chicken broth, skim milk, green onions, bell pepper, lemon rind and black pepper in a deep 3-quart microwave-safe casserole dish; cover with microwaveable plastic wrap and microwave on HIGH 5 to 6 minutes, or until thoroughly heated. Stir in instant potatoes. Cover and microwave on HIGH 1 to 2 minutes, or until heated. Stir well; serve immediately.   *Makes 4 servings*

New England Clam Chowder

Shrimp and Fish Gumbo

½ pound fresh or thawed frozen orange roughy or other fish fillets
3¾ cups water, divided
6 ounces medium raw shrimp, peeled
1 cup chopped onion
½ cup chopped green bell pepper
2 cloves garlic, minced
½ teaspoon fish or chicken bouillon granules
2 cans (about 14 ounces each) stewed tomatoes, drained
1½ cups frozen okra, thawed
1 teaspoon dried thyme
1 teaspoon dried savory
¼ teaspoon ground red pepper
⅛ teaspoon black pepper
2 tablespoons cornstarch
2 cups hot cooked brown rice

1. Cut fish into 1-inch pieces. Bring 3 cups water to a boil in medium saucepan over high heat. Add fish and shrimp; cook 3 to 4 minutes or until fish begins to flake when tested with fork and shrimp are pink and opaque. Drain; set aside.

2. Combine onion, bell pepper, ½ cup water, garlic and bouillon in large saucepan. Bring to a boil over medium-high heat. Reduce heat to medium-low; cover and simmer 2 to 3 minutes or until vegetables are crisp-tender.

3. Stir in tomatoes, okra, thyme, savory, red pepper and black pepper; return to a boil. Reduce heat; simmer, uncovered, 3 to 5 minutes or until okra is tender.

4. Stir remaining ¼ cup water into cornstarch in small bowl until smooth. Stir into gumbo until blended; cook and stir until mixture boils and thickens. Add fish, shrimp and ham; cook until heated through. Serve over rice.

Makes 4 servings

Tomato-Basil Crab Bisque

　1 tablespoon butter
½ cup chopped onion
　1 can (8 ounces) HUNT'S® Tomato Sauce with Roasted Garlic
　1 cup half-and-half
　1 cup coarsely chopped cooked crabmeat
½ cup chicken broth
¼ teaspoon salt
⅛ teaspoon ground black pepper
¼ cup chopped fresh basil leaves

1. Melt butter in a medium saucepan over medium-high heat. Add onion; cook 3 minutes or until tender, stirring frequently.

2. Add tomato sauce, half-and-half, crabmeat, broth, salt and pepper. Bring just to a boil; reduce heat to low. Cover tightly and simmer 5 minutes. Sprinkle with basil before serving.

Makes 4 servings

Simple Seafood Soup

2½ cups water or chicken broth
1½ cups dry white wine
　1 onion, chopped
½ red bell pepper, chopped
½ green bell pepper, chopped
　1 clove garlic, minced
½ pound halibut, cut into 1-inch chunks
½ pound sea scallops, cut into halves
　1 teaspoon dried thyme
　　Juice of ½ lime
　　Dash hot pepper sauce
　　Salt and black pepper

1. Combine water, wine, onion, bell peppers and garlic in large saucepan; bring to a boil. Reduce heat to medium-low; cover and simmer 15 minutes or until bell peppers are tender, stirring occasionally.

2. Add fish, scallops and thyme; cook 2 minutes or until fish and scallops turn opaque. Stir in lime juice and hot pepper sauce. Season with salt and black pepper. *Makes 4 servings*

Tomato-Basil Crab Bisque

Cioppino

2 tablespoons olive or vegetable oil

1½ cups chopped onions

1 cup chopped celery

½ cup chopped green bell pepper

1 clove garlic, minced

1 can (28 ounces) CONTADINA® Recipe Ready Original Crushed Tomatoes

1 can (6 ounces) CONTADINA® Tomato Paste

1 teaspoon Italian herb seasoning

1 teaspoon salt

½ teaspoon ground black pepper

2 cups water

1 cup dry red wine or chicken broth

3 pounds clams, oysters, cooked crab, cooked lobster, whitefish, scallops and/or shrimp (in any proportion)

1. Heat oil in large saucepan. Add onions, celery, bell pepper and garlic; sauté until vegetables are tender. Add tomatoes, tomato paste, Italian seasoning, salt, black pepper, water and wine.

2. Bring to a boil. Reduce heat to low; simmer, uncovered, for 15 minutes.

3. To prepare fish and seafood: scrub clams and oysters under running water. Place in ½ inch boiling water in separate large saucepan; cover. Bring to a boil. Reduce heat to low; simmer just until shells open, about 3 minutes. Set aside.

4. Cut crab, lobster, fish and scallops into bite-size pieces. Shell and devein shrimp.

5. Add fish to tomato mixture; simmer 5 minutes. Add scallops and shrimp; simmer 5 minutes.

6. Add crab, lobster and reserved clams and oysters; simmer until heated through.

Makes about 14 cups

Prep Time: 30 minutes
Cook Time: 35 minutes

Tortilla Soup with Grouper

1 tablespoon vegetable oil
1 onion, chopped
2 cloves garlic, minced
3½ cups chicken broth
1½ cups tomato juice
1 cup chopped tomatoes
1 can (4 ounces) diced green chiles, drained
2 teaspoons Worcestershire sauce
1 teaspoon salt
1 teaspoon ground cumin
1 teaspoon chili powder
⅛ teaspoon black pepper
3 corn tortillas, cut into 1-inch strips
1 cup corn
1 pound grouper fillets, cut into 1-inch cubes
Fresh parsley sprigs and jalapeño pepper rings (optional)

1. Heat oil in large saucepan over medium-high heat. Add onion and garlic; cook and stir until softened.

2. Stir in broth, tomato juice, tomatoes, chiles, Worcestershire sauce, salt, cumin, chili powder and pepper; bring to a boil. Reduce heat to medium-low; cover and simmer 10 minutes.

3. Add tortillas and corn. Simmer, covered, 8 to 10 minutes.

4. Stir in grouper. Simmer, uncovered, until fish begins to flake when tested with fork.

5. Garnish with parsley and jalapeño pepper. Serve immediately.   *Makes 6 servings*

Shrimp and Pepper Bisque

1 bag (12 ounces) frozen stir-fry vegetables, thawed
½ pound frozen cauliflower florets, thawed
1 stalk celery, sliced
1 tablespoon seafood seasoning
½ teaspoon dried thyme
1 can (about 14 ounces) chicken broth
12 ounces medium raw shrimp, peeled
2 cups half-and-half
2 to 3 green onions, finely chopped

Slow Cooker Directions

1. Combine stir-fry vegetables, cauliflower, celery, seasoning and thyme in slow cooker. Pour in broth. Cover; cook on LOW 8 hours or on HIGH 4 hours.

2. Stir in shrimp. Cover; cook 15 minutes or until shrimp are pink and opaque. Working in batches, process soup in food processor or blender until smooth; return to slow cooker. Stir in half-and-half; cook until heated through. Sprinkle with green onions just before serving.

Makes 4 servings

Tip: For a creamier, smoother consistency, strain through several layers of damp cheesecloth.

New Orleans Fish Soup

1 pound skinless firm fish fillets, such as grouper, cod or haddock
1 can (about 15 ounces) cannellini beans, rinsed and drained
1 can (about 14 ounces) chicken broth
1 yellow squash, halved lengthwise and sliced
1 tablespoon Cajun seasoning
2 cans (about 14 ounces each) stewed tomatoes
½ cup sliced green onions
1 teaspoon grated orange peel

1. Cut fish into 1-inch pieces. Combine beans, broth, squash and seasoning in large saucepan; bring to a boil over high heat.

2. Stir in tomatoes and fish. Reduce heat to medium-low; cover and simmer 3 to 5 minutes or until fish just begins to flake when tested with fork. Stir in green onions and orange peel.

Makes 4 servings

Shrimp and Pepper Bisque

Crab and Corn Chowder

    4 slices bacon
    1 large sweet onion, coarsely chopped (about 2 cups)
    2 cloves garlic, minced
    6 cups SWANSON® Chicken Broth (Regular, Natural Goodness® or Certified Organic)
    2 teaspoons seafood seasoning
    6 to 8 red potatoes or fingerling potatoes, cut into 1-inch pieces (about 2 cups)
    2 cups frozen whole kernel corn
    1 container (8 ounces) refrigerated pasteurized lump crabmeat
½ cup heavy cream

1. Cook the bacon in a 4-quart saucepan over medium-high heat for 5 minutes or until it's crisp. Remove the bacon with a fork or kitchen tongs and drain on paper towels. Crumble the bacon and set aside. Pour off all but **2 tablespoons** drippings.

2. Reduce the heat to medium. Add the onion and garlic to the saucepan and cook until the onion is tender.

3. Stir in the broth, seafood seasoning, potatoes and corn. Heat to a boil. Reduce the heat to low. Cook for 15 minutes or until the potatoes are tender.

4. Stir in the crabmeat and cream and cook for 5 minutes or until the mixture is hot and bubbling. Divide the chowder among **6** serving bowls. Top **each** with **about 1 tablespoon** bacon. *Makes 6 servings*

Prep Time: 15 minutes
Cook Time: 35 minutes

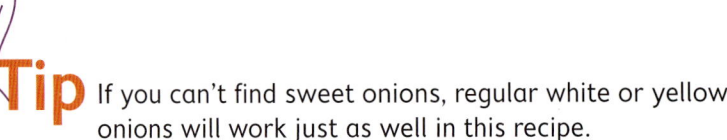 **Tip** If you can't find sweet onions, regular white or yellow onions will work just as well in this recipe.

GLOBAL GOURMET

Spicy Thai Shrimp Soup

  1 tablespoon vegetable oil
  1 pound medium raw shrimp, peeled, shells reserved
  1 jalapeño pepper,* cut into slivers
  1 tablespoon paprika
  ¼ teaspoon ground red pepper
  4 cans (about 14 ounces each) chicken broth
  1 (½-inch) strip *each* lemon and lime peel
  1 can (15 ounces) straw mushrooms, drained
    Juice of 1 lemon
    Juice of 1 lime
  2 tablespoons soy sauce
  1 red Thai pepper,* red jalapeño pepper* *or* ¼ small red bell pepper, cut into strips
  ¼ cup fresh cilantro leaves

These peppers can sting and irritate the skin, so wear rubber gloves when handling peppers and do not touch your eyes.

1. Heat large skillet or wok over medium-high heat 1 minute. Add oil; heat 30 seconds. Add shrimp and jalapeño pepper slivers; stir-fry 1 minute. Add paprika and ground red pepper; stir-fry 1 minute or until shrimp are pink and opaque. Transfer shrimp mixture to medium bowl; set aside.

2. Add shrimp shells to skillet; stir-fry 30 seconds. Add broth and lemon and lime peels; bring to a boil. Reduce heat to low; cover and simmer 15 minutes.

3. Remove shells and peels with slotted spoon; discard. Add mushrooms and shrimp mixture to broth; bring to a boil. Stir in lemon and lime juices, soy sauce and Thai pepper. Ladle soup into bowls. Sprinkle with cilantro. Serve immediately.   *Makes 6 servings*

Chicken Tortilla and Rice Soup

   2 cups MINUTE® White Rice, uncooked
   5 cups low-sodium chicken broth
   1 cup carrots, peeled and sliced thin
   1 can (10 ounces) diced tomatoes with green chiles
   1 cup (6 ounces) cooked chicken breast, cubed
   1 tablespoon lime juice (optional)
  20 baked tortilla chips (about 1 cup), slightly crushed
  ½ cup low-fat Mexican cheese blend, shredded
  ¼ cup fresh cilantro, chopped
   1 avocado, diced (optional)

Prepare rice according to package directions.

Bring broth to a boil in medium pot. Reduce heat and add carrots, tomatoes with chiles and chicken; simmer 10 minutes.

Stir in rice; add lime juice, if desired. Divide equally into 6 serving bowls and top with tortilla chips, cheese, cilantro and avocado, if desired.   *Makes 6 servings*

Tip To dice an avocado, insert a knife into the stem end. Slice in half lengthwise to the pit, turning the avocado while slicing. Twist the halves in opposite directions to pull apart. Press the knife blade into the pit, twisting gently to pull the pit away from the avocado. Discard the pit. Cut the avocado flesh in a crisscross fashion, then run a spoon underneath to scoop out the pieces.

Egg Drop Soup

4 cups chicken broth
2 tablespoons soy sauce
1 tablespoon dry sherry
1 tablespoon water
1 tablespoon cornstarch
2 eggs, well beaten
2 green onions, thinly sliced diagonally
2 teaspoons dark sesame oil

1. Combine broth, soy sauce and sherry in large saucepan; bring to a boil over high heat. Reduce heat to low; simmer 2 minutes.

2. Stir water into cornstarch in small bowl until smooth. Stir into soup until blended; simmer 3 minutes or until slightly thickened.

3. Stirring constantly in one direction, slowly add eggs to soup in thin stream. Stir in green onions. Remove from heat; stir in sesame oil. Serve immediately.   *Makes 4 servings*

Hungarian Bean & Veg•All® Soup

3 cups chicken broth
3 cups water
1 pound smoked pork shank or hock
1 small turnip, diced (about 1 cup)
2 cans (1 pound each) of Allens White Beans (Navy or Cannellini), rinsed and drained
1 can (15 ounces) VEG•ALL® Original Mixed Vegetables, drained
2 tablespoons butter
2 tablespoons flour
1 tablespoon paprika
²/₃ cup sour cream

Combine chicken broth, water and pork shank in medium pot and bring to a boil. Reduce heat and simmer 30 minutes. Remove shank, cut meat into bite-size pieces, and return them to pot. Add turnips and simmer 15 minutes longer, then add white beans and Veg•All.

In medium skillet, melt butter and beat in flour, cooking until roux just begins to brown. Stir in paprika and sour cream. Stir in enough of the soup to liquefy the mixture, then pour it back into remaining soup in pot. Taste for seasoning and serve immediately.   *Makes 8 servings*

Albondigas Soup

  1 pound ground beef
  2 eggs, lightly beaten
¼ cup blue or yellow cornmeal
  1 clove garlic, minced
  1 tablespoon chopped fresh mint *or* 1 teaspoon crumbled dried mint
½ teaspoon salt
¼ teaspoon ground cumin
    Dash black pepper
  6 cups water
  3 cans (10½ ounces each) condensed beef broth, undiluted
  1 onion, chopped
¼ cup sliced celery
  1 carrot, chopped
  1 zucchini, chopped
  1 yellow squash, chopped
½ bunch spinach, stemmed and sliced ½ inch thick
  2 limes, cut into wedges

1. Combine beef, eggs, cornmeal, garlic, mint, salt, cumin and pepper in medium bowl. Shape mixture into 1-inch balls; set aside.

2. Combine water, broth, onion and celery in large saucepan or Dutch oven; bring to a boil over high heat. Reduce heat to medium-low; simmer 10 minutes.

3. Add meatballs to broth mixture; simmer 5 minutes. Spoon off fat and foam from surface of broth. Add carrot, zucchini and squash; simmer 20 minutes or until vegetables are tender.

4. Add spinach; simmer 5 minutes or until wilted. Serve with lime wedges.

Makes 6 servings

Thai Coconut Soup

  2 cups chicken broth
  1 can (13½ ounces) light coconut milk
  1 tablespoon minced fresh ginger
½ to 1 teaspoon red curry paste
  3 cups coarsely shredded cooked chicken (about 12 ounces)
  1 can (15 ounces) straw mushrooms, drained
  1 can (about 8 ounces) baby corn, drained
  2 tablespoons lime juice
¼ cup chopped fresh cilantro

Combine broth, coconut milk, ginger and red curry paste in large saucepan. Add chicken, mushrooms and corn. Bring to a simmer over medium heat; cook until heated through. Stir in lime juice. Sprinkle with cilantro before serving.   *Makes 4 servings*

Note: Red curry paste can be found in jars in the Asian food section of large grocery stores. Spice levels can vary between brands. Start with ½ teaspoon, then add more as desired.

Greek Lemon and Rice Soup

  3 cans (about 14 ounces each) chicken broth
½ cup uncooked long grain rice
  3 egg yolks
¼ cup fresh lemon juice
    Salt and black pepper
  4 thin slices lemon (optional)
  4 teaspoons finely chopped fresh Italian parsley (optional)

Slow Cooker Directions

1. Stir together broth and rice in slow cooker. Cover; cook on HIGH 2 to 3 hours or until rice is tender.

2. *Turn slow cooker to LOW.* Whisk together egg yolks and lemon juice in medium bowl. Add large spoonful of hot rice mixture to egg yolk mixture and whisk together briefly, then whisk this mixture back into slow cooker. Cover; cook 10 minutes.

3. Season with salt and pepper. Garnish with lemon slices and parsley.   *Makes 4 servings*

French Onion Soup

    1 tablespoon vegetable oil
    2 large onions, cut in half and thinly sliced (about 2 cups)
1/4 teaspoon sugar
    2 tablespoons all-purpose flour
    4 cups SWANSON® Beef Broth (Regular, 50% Less Sodium or Certified Organic)
1/4 cup dry white wine or dry vermouth
    4 slices French bread, toasted
1/2 cup shredded Swiss cheese

1. Heat the oil in a 6-quart saucepot over low heat. Add the onions. Cover and cook for 15 minutes. Uncover the saucepot.

2. Add the sugar to the saucepot and increase the heat to medium. Cook for 15 minutes or until the onions are golden.

3. Stir in the flour. Cook and stir for 1 minute. Add the broth and wine. Heat to a boil. Reduce the heat to low. Cook for 10 minutes.

4. Divide the soup among **4** serving bowls. Top **each** with **1** bread slice and **2 tablespoons** cheese.

Makes 4 servings

Kitchen Tip: For added flavor, rub the bread with a peeled garlic clove before toasting.

Prep Time: 10 minutes
Cook Time: 45 minutes

Beef Goulash Soup with Caraway

1¼ pounds boneless beef sirloin tri-tip roast*
1 teaspoon canola oil
1 cup chopped onion
3 cans (about 14 ounces each) beef broth
2 cans (about 14 ounces each) diced tomatoes
1½ cups sliced carrots
2 tablespoons sugar
1 tablespoon paprika
1 tablespoon caraway seeds, slightly crushed
2 cloves garlic, minced
4 ounces (about 2 cups) uncooked whole wheat noodles
2 cups thinly sliced cabbage or coleslaw mix

Substitute chuck roast or beef round steak, if desired.

1. Trim fat from beef and discard. Cut beef into 1-inch pieces.

2. Heat oil in nonstick Dutch oven over medium heat. Brown beef in 2 batches; transfer to paper towel-lined plate. Drain all but 1 tablespoon fat. Add onion; cook 3 minutes or until onion is tender, stirring occasionally.

3. Return beef to Dutch oven. Add broth, tomatoes, carrots, sugar, paprika, caraway seeds and garlic; bring to a boil. Reduce heat to medium-low; cover and simmer 45 minutes or until beef is tender.

4. Stir in noodles; bring to a boil. Reduce heat to medium-low; simmer, uncovered, 10 minutes or until noodles are tender. Stir in cabbage; simmer 2 minutes or until heated through.

Makes 6 to 8 servings

Creamy Tuscan Bean & Chicken Soup

2 cans (10¾ ounces each) **CAMPBELL'S®** Condensed Cream of Celery Soup (Regular or 98% Fat Free)

2 cups water

1 can (about 15 ounces) white kidney beans (cannellini), rinsed and drained

1 can (about 14½ ounces) diced tomatoes, undrained

2 cups shredded or diced cooked chicken

¼ cup bacon bits

3 ounces fresh baby spinach leaves (about 3 cups)

Olive oil

Grated or shredded Parmesan cheese

1. Heat the soup, water, beans, tomatoes, chicken and bacon in a 3-quart saucepan over medium-high heat to a boil.

2. Stir in the spinach. Cook for 5 minutes or until the spinach is wilted. Serve the soup with a drizzle of oil and sprinkle with the cheese.   *Makes 4 to 6 servings*

Prep Time: 10 minutes
Cook Time: 10 minutes

Tip For the shredded chicken, purchase a rotisserie chicken. Remove the skin and bones. You can either shred the chicken with your fingers or use 2 forks.

Pork and Noodle Soup

    1 package (1 ounce) dried shiitake mushrooms
    4 ounces thin egg noodles or spaghetti
    6 cups chicken broth
    2 cloves garlic, minced
 ½ cup shredded carrots
    4 ounces ham or Canadian bacon, cut into short thin strips
    1 tablespoon hoisin sauce
 ⅛ teaspoon black pepper
    2 tablespoons minced fresh chives

1. Place mushrooms in small bowl; cover with warm water. Soak 20 minutes to soften. Drain; squeeze out excess water. Discard stems; slice caps.

2. Meanwhile, cook noodles according to package directions until tender. Drain and set aside.

3. Combine broth and garlic in large saucepan; bring to a boil over high heat. Reduce heat to low. Add mushrooms, carrots, ham, hoisin sauce and pepper to saucepan. Simmer 15 minutes. Stir in noodles; simmer until heated through. Sprinkle with chives just before serving.

Makes 4 to 6 servings

Middle Eastern Chicken Soup

    1 can (about 14 ounces) chicken broth
    1 can (about 15 ounces) chickpeas, rinsed and drained
    1 cup chopped cooked chicken
    1 onion, chopped
    1 carrot, chopped
    1 clove garlic, minced
    1 teaspoon *each* dried oregano and ground cumin
 ½ (10-ounce) package fresh spinach, stemmed and coarsely chopped
 ⅛ teaspoon black pepper

Combine broth, 1½ cans water, chickpeas, chicken, onion, carrot, garlic, oregano and cumin in medium saucepan. Bring to a boil over high heat. Reduce heat to medium-low; cover and simmer 15 minutes. Stir in spinach and pepper; simmer, uncovered, 2 minutes or until wilted.

Makes 4 servings

French Peasant Soup

   1 slice bacon, chopped
¹⁄₂ cup diced carrots
¹⁄₂ cup diced celery
¹⁄₄ cup minced onion
   1 clove garlic, minced
   2 tablespoons white wine or water
   1 can (about 14 ounces) vegetable broth
   1 sprig fresh thyme *or* **1** teaspoon dried thyme
   1 bay leaf
   1 sprig fresh parsley *or* **1** teaspoon dried parsley
¹⁄₂ cup chopped green beans
   2 tablespoons uncooked small pasta or elbow macaroni
¹⁄₂ cup canned cannellini beans, rinsed and drained
¹⁄₂ cup diced zucchini
¹⁄₄ cup chopped leek
   2 teaspoons prepared pesto sauce
   2 teaspoons grated Parmesan cheese

1. Cook bacon in medium saucepan over medium heat 3 minutes or until partially cooked. Add carrots, celery, onion and garlic; cook 5 minutes or until carrots are crisp-tender.

2. Stir in wine; simmer until most of wine has evaporated. Add broth, thyme, bay leaf and parsley; simmer 10 minutes.

3. Add green beans; simmer 5 minutes. Add pasta; cook 5 to 7 minutes or until almost tender.

4. Add cannellini beans, zucchini and leek; cook 3 to 5 minutes or until vegetables are tender.

5. Remove and discard bay leaf. Ladle soup into two bowls. Stir 1 teaspoon pesto into each bowl and sprinkle with 1 teaspoon cheese.   *Makes 2 servings*

Hot and Sour Soup

    1 package (1 ounce) dried shiitake mushrooms
    4 ounces firm tofu, drained
    4 cups chicken broth
    3 tablespoons white vinegar
    2 tablespoons soy sauce
    ½ to 1 teaspoon hot chili oil
    ¼ teaspoon white pepper
    1 cup shredded cooked pork, chicken or turkey
    ½ cup drained canned bamboo shoots, cut into thin strips
    3 tablespoons water
    2 tablespoons cornstarch
    1 egg white, lightly beaten
    ¼ cup thinly sliced green onions or chopped fresh cilantro
    1 teaspoon dark sesame oil

1. Place mushrooms in small bowl; cover with warm water. Soak 20 minutes to soften. Drain; squeeze out excess water. Discard stems; slice caps.

2. Press tofu lightly between paper towels; cut into ½-inch squares or triangles.

3. Combine broth, vinegar, soy sauce, chili oil and white pepper in medium saucepan. Bring to a boil over high heat. Reduce heat to medium-low; simmer 2 minutes.

4. Stir in mushrooms, tofu, pork and bamboo shoots; cook and stir until heated through.

5. Stir water into cornstarch in small bowl until smooth. Add to soup; stir until blended. Cook and stir 4 minutes or until soup boils and thickens. Remove from heat.

6. Stirring constantly in one direction, slowly pour egg white in thin stream into soup. Stir in green onions and sesame oil. Ladle into soup bowls.

Makes 4 servings

TABLE OF CONTENTS

PERFECT POULTRY

Teriyaki Chicken and Vegetables

12 TYSON® Individually Frozen Chicken Breast Tenderloins
1 tablespoon vegetable oil
2½ cups broccoli florets (about 8 ounces)
⅔ cup water
1 can (15 ounces) baby corn, drained
1 can (15 ounces) straw mushrooms, drained
⅔ cup bottled thick sweet-and-sour sauce
⅓ cup cashews or peanuts
4 cups hot cooked white rice

1. Wash hands. Remove protective ice glaze from frozen tenderloins by holding under lukewarm running water about 1 minute. Pat dry. Wash hands.

2. Heat oil in large skillet over medium heat. Add chicken; cover and cook, turning occasionally, 10 to 12 minutes or until browned and internal juices of chicken run clear. (Or insert instant-read meat thermometer into thickest part of chicken. Temperature should read 180°F.) Transfer chicken to plate; cover and keep warm.

3. Add broccoli and water to skillet; cover immediately and cook 3 minutes over medium heat. Add chicken (and any accumulated juices), corn, mushrooms and sweet-and-sour sauce to skillet. Heat thoroughly. Stir in cashews. Serve over cooked rice. Refrigerate leftovers immediately. *Makes 6 servings*

Prep Time: 5 minutes
Cook Time: 18 minutes

Skillet Lasagna with Vegetables

½ pound hot Italian turkey sausage
½ pound ground turkey
2 stalks celery, sliced
⅓ cup chopped onion
2 cups marinara sauce
1⅓ cups water
4 ounces uncooked farfalle (bow tie) pasta
1 zucchini, halved lengthwise and cut into ½-inch-thick slices
¾ cup chopped green or yellow bell pepper
½ cup ricotta cheese
2 tablespoons finely shredded Parmesan cheese
½ cup (2 ounces) shredded mozzarella cheese

1. Remove sausage from casing. Cook and stir sausage, turkey, celery and onion in large skillet over medium-high heat until turkey is no longer pink. Stir in marinara sauce and water. Bring to a boil. Stir in pasta. Reduce heat to medium-low; cover and simmer 12 minutes.

2. Add zucchini and bell pepper; simmer, covered, 2 minutes. Uncover; simmer 2 to 6 minutes or until vegetables are crisp-tender.

3. Meanwhile, combine ricotta and Parmesan cheese in small bowl. Drop by rounded teaspoonfuls on top of mixture in skillet. Sprinkle mozzarella cheese over top. Remove from heat; cover and let stand 10 minutes.   *Makes 4 to 6 servings*

Prep and Cook Time: 30 minutes

Zesty Chicken Succotash

    1 (3- to 4-pound) chicken, cut up and skinned, if desired
    1 onion, chopped
    1 rib celery, sliced
  ¼ cup *Frank's® RedHot®* Original Cayenne Pepper Sauce
 1½ cups frozen lima beans
    1 package (10 ounces) frozen whole kernel corn
    2 tomatoes, coarsely chopped

1. Heat *1 tablespoon oil* in large skillet until hot. Add chicken; cook 10 minutes or until browned on all sides. Drain off all but 1 tablespoon fat. Add onion and celery; cook and stir 3 minutes or until tender.

2. Stir in *¾ cup water,* **Frank's RedHot** Sauce and remaining ingredients. Heat to boiling. Reduce heat to medium-low. Cook, covered, 20 to 25 minutes or until chicken is no longer pink near bone. Sprinkle with chopped fresh parsley, if desired.   *Makes 6 servings*

Prep Time: 10 minutes
Cook Time: 35 minutes

Chicken With Artichokes

    2 jars (6 ounces each) marinated artichoke hearts packed in oil
    6 skinless, boneless chicken breast halves
    1 jar (1 pound 10 ounces) PREGO® Onion & Garlic or Traditional Italian Sauce
    6 slices prosciutto or salami (about 2 ounces)
    6 slices provolone cheese (about 4 ounces)
      Hot cooked rice-shaped pasta (orzo)

1. Drain the artichokes, reserving **1 tablespoon** of the oil.

2. Heat the reserved oil in a 12-inch skillet over medium-high heat. Add the chicken and cook for 10 minutes or until it's well browned on both sides. Add the artichokes and cook for 1 minute.

3. Add the sauce to the skillet and reduce the heat to medium. Cover and cook for 5 minutes or until the chicken is cooked through.

4. Top each chicken breast with **1 slice each** prosciutto and cheese. Cover and cook for 2 minutes or until the cheese melts. Serve with the pasta.   *Makes 6 servings*

Zesty Chicken Succotash

Chicken with Pomegranate-Orange Sauce

2 tablespoons soy sauce, divided
3 teaspoons cornstarch, divided
1 pound boneless skinless chicken breasts, cut into 1-inch cubes
½ cup pomegranate juice
1 to 2 tablespoons chili garlic sauce
1 teaspoon grated orange peel
1 teaspoon grated fresh ginger
1 tablespoon vegetable or peanut oil
2 stalks celery, cut diagonally into ¼-inch slices
1 red bell pepper, cut into 1-inch-long strips
2 oranges, peeled and sectioned
3 green onions, sliced
2 cups hot cooked rice

1. Stir 1 tablespoon soy sauce into 1 teaspoon cornstarch in medium bowl until smooth. Add chicken; toss to coat. Cover; let stand 10 minutes.

2. Meanwhile, combine pomegranate juice, chili garlic sauce, remaining 1 tablespoon soy sauce, remaining 2 teaspoons cornstarch, orange peel and ginger in small bowl; stir until blended.

3. Heat oil in large nonstick skillet over medium-high heat. Add chicken; stir-fry 2 minutes. Add celery and bell pepper; stir-fry 3 minutes or until chicken is cooked through.

4. Stir pomegranate juice mixture; add to skillet. Bring to a boil over high heat. Reduce heat to medium-low; simmer 1 minute. Gently stir in orange sections; cook until heated through. Sprinkle with green onions; serve with rice. *Makes 4 servings*

Creamy Bow-Tie Pasta with Chicken and Broccoli

3 cups (8 ounces) farfalle (bow-tie pasta), uncooked
4 cups broccoli florets
3 tablespoons KRAFT® Roasted Red Pepper Italian with Parmesan Dressing
6 small boneless, skinless chicken breast halves (1½ pounds)
2 cloves garlic, minced
2 cups tomato-basil spaghetti sauce
4 ounces (½ of 8-ounce package) PHILADELPHIA® Neufchâtel Cheese, ⅓ Less Fat than Cream Cheese, cubed
¼ cup KRAFT® 100% Grated Parmesan Cheese

1. Cook pasta as directed on package, adding broccoli to the cooking water for the last 3 minutes of the pasta cooking time. Meanwhile, heat dressing in large nonstick skillet on medium heat. Add chicken and garlic; cook 5 minutes. Turn chicken over; continue cooking 4 to 5 minutes or until chicken is cooked through (170°F).

2. Drain pasta mixture in colander; return to pan and set aside. Add spaghetti sauce and Neufchâtel cheese to chicken in skillet; cook on medium-low heat 2 to 3 minutes or until Neufchâtel cheese is completely melted, mixture is well blended and chicken is coated with sauce, stirring occasionally. Remove chicken from skillet; keep warm. Add sauce mixture to pasta mixture; mix well. Transfer to six serving bowls.

3. Cut chicken crosswise into thick slices; fan out chicken over pasta mixture. Sprinkle evenly with Parmesan cheese.   *Makes 6 servings*

Prep Time: 10 minutes
Cook Time: 15 minutes

Sautéed Chicken with Pears

4 TYSON® Fresh Boneless Skinless Chicken Breasts
4 tablespoons low-sodium soy sauce
¾ cup orange juice, divided
½ cup sliced celery
3 green onions, sliced
½ pound sugar snap peas
2 red Bartlett pears, cored, sliced lengthwise, then cut in half
Salt and black pepper, to taste

1. Wash hands. Spray large skillet with nonstick cooking spray. Put chicken in skillet. Wash hands. In small bowl, combine soy sauce and ¼ cup orange juice; pour over chicken. Cook, turning after 3 minutes, 6 to 7 minutes or until internal juices of chicken run clear. (Or insert instant-read meat thermometer into thickest part of chicken. Temperature should read 180°F.) Remove chicken; cover and keep warm.

2. Add celery and onions to skillet; cook 2 minutes. Stir in peas and pears and cook 3 more minutes. Return chicken to skillet and add remaining ½ cup orange juice, salt and pepper. Cook 2 minutes or until heated thoroughly. Refrigerate leftovers immediately.

Makes 4 servings

Chicken and Veggies in Cajun Cream

3 cups TYSON® Frozen Fully Cooked Grilled Chicken Breast Strips
1 red bell pepper, cut into ¼-inch strips
1 bag (1 pound) frozen vegetable blend with pasta
¼ cup water
½ cup whipping cream
1 teaspoon cumin
⅛ teaspoon ground red pepper

Spray large skillet with nonstick cooking spray. Heat over medium-high heat. Add chicken and bell pepper strips; cook and stir 2 minutes. Add frozen vegetables with pasta and water to skillet. Stir while bringing to a boil; simmer 2 minutes. Stir in cream, cumin and red pepper. Cover; cook, stirring occasionally, until sauce is thickened and pasta is done to taste (5 to 8 minutes). Refrigerate leftovers immediately.

Makes 6 servings

Prep Time: 5 minutes
Cook Time: 15 minutes

Sautéed Chicken with Pears

Spanish Braised Chicken with Green Olives and Rice

    2 pounds bone-in skinless chicken thighs
    1 teaspoon paprika
      Nonstick cooking spray
   ¾ cup dry sherry
 2¼ cups water
    1 can (about 14 ounces) chicken broth
   ¾ cup sliced pimiento-stuffed green olives
 1½ teaspoons dried sage
 1½ cups uncooked long grain white rice

1. Sprinkle chicken thighs with paprika. Spray large nonstick skillet with cooking spray; heat over medium-high heat. Cook chicken 6 to 8 minutes or until browned on both sides, turning once.

2. Remove chicken from skillet. Add sherry, stirring to scrape up browned bits from bottom of skillet. Add water, broth, olives and sage; bring to a boil.

3. Reduce heat to low. Return chicken to skillet. Cover and simmer 10 minutes.

4. Add rice to liquid around chicken; gently stir to distribute evenly in skillet. Cover; simmer 20 to 25 minutes or until rice is tender and chicken is cooked through (165°F).

Makes 6 servings

 **Tip** Leftover opened jars of olives should be kept refrigerated in their brine or oil in a tightly covered container. Olives will keep for several weeks. When the olives begin to turn soft, discard them.

Spanish Braised Chicken with Green Olives and Rice

Chicken-Orzo Skillet

 1 tablespoon olive oil
 1 teaspoon Greek seasoning *or* 1 teaspoon oregano plus dash garlic powder
 ½ teaspoon *each* grated lemon peel and black pepper
 4 boneless skinless chicken breasts (about 1½ pounds), cut into 1-inch cubes
 1 can (about 14 ounces) chicken broth
1¼ cups uncooked orzo pasta
 6 ounces Greek green olives, drained
 4 cloves garlic, minced
 2 cups packed torn stemmed spinach
 ½ cup crumbled feta cheese, plus additional for garnish

1. Heat oil in large nonstick skillet over medium heat. Add seasoning, lemon peel and pepper; cook and stir just until fragrant. Add chicken; cook and stir 4 minutes.

2. Stir in broth, orzo, olives and garlic. Bring to a boil. Reduce heat to medium-low; simmer, partially covered, 15 minutes or until pasta is tender and chicken is cooked through, stirring occasionally.

3. Stir in spinach and feta. Cover; let stand 2 to 3 minutes or until spinach wilts. Garnish with additional feta.   *Makes 4 servings*

Broccoli Chicken Potato Parmesan

 2 tablespoons vegetable oil
 1 pound small red potatoes, sliced ¼-inch thick
 1 can (10¾ ounces) CAMPBELL'S® Condensed Broccoli Cheese Soup
 ½ cup milk
 ¼ teaspoon garlic powder
 2 cups fresh *or* frozen broccoli flowerets
 1 package (about 10 ounces) refrigerated cooked chicken breast strips
 ¼ cup grated Parmesan cheese

1. Heat the oil in a 10-inch skillet over medium heat. Add the potatoes. Cover and cook for 10 minutes, stirring occasionally.

2. Stir the soup, milk, garlic powder, broccoli and chicken into the skillet. Sprinkle with the cheese. Heat to a boil. Reduce heat to low. Cover and cook for 5 minutes or until the potatoes are fork-tender.   *Makes 4 servings*

Chicken-Orzo Skillet

Smothered Chicken

6 boneless skinless chicken breasts, cut into ¾-inch cubes
1½ cups finely chopped vegetables (onion, celery and green bell pepper)
3 cloves garlic, minced
1 can (14½ ounces) stewed tomatoes, undrained
1 can (10¾ ounces) condensed golden mushroom soup, undiluted
3 tablespoons *French's*® Worcestershire Sauce

1. Melt *2 tablespoons butter* in large nonstick skillet over medium-high heat. Add chicken; cook and stir 5 minutes or until well browned. Add vegetables and garlic; cook and stir 3 minutes.

2. Stir in tomatoes with liquid, soup and Worcestershire. Heat to boiling. Reduce heat to medium-low; cook 2 minutes.
Makes 6 servings

Prep Time: 15 minutes
Cook Time: 10 minutes

Southwestern Chicken and Black Bean Skillet

1 teaspoon ground cumin
1 teaspoon chili powder
½ teaspoon salt
4 boneless skinless chicken breasts
2 teaspoons canola or vegetable oil
1 cup chopped onion
1 red bell pepper, chopped
1 can (about 15 ounces) black beans, rinsed and drained
½ cup chunky salsa
¼ cup chopped fresh cilantro or thinly sliced green onions (optional)

1. Combine cumin, chili powder and salt in small bowl; sprinkle evenly over both sides of chicken. Heat oil in large nonstick skillet over medium-high heat. Add chicken; cook 4 minutes, turning once. Transfer chicken to plate.

2. Add onion to same skillet; cook and stir 1 minute. Add bell pepper; cook 5 minutes, stirring occasionally. Stir in beans and salsa.

3. Place chicken on top of bean mixture. Cover and cook 6 to 7 minutes or until chicken is no longer pink in center. Garnish with cilantro.
Makes 4 servings

Smothered Chicken

BOUNTIFUL BEEF

Classic Beef Stroganoff

1 cup MINUTE® White Rice, uncooked
1 tablespoon vegetable oil
1 cup onion, chopped
1 pound lean ground beef
2 cups mushrooms, sliced
1 can (14½ ounces) beef broth
1 can (10¾ ounces) cream of mushroom soup
1 tablespoon Worcestershire sauce
½ cup sour cream

Prepare rice according to package directions.

Heat oil in medium skillet over medium-high heat. Add onion; cook and stir 3 minutes. Add beef and brown; drain excess fat.

Add mushrooms, broth, soup and Worcestershire sauce. Bring to a boil and simmer 5 minutes. Stir in sour cream. Serve over rice. *Makes 4 servings*

Mexican Linguine

    1 pound lean ground beef
    1 small onion, chopped
    1 jar (16 ounces) ORTEGA® Garden Vegetable Salsa
    1 cup whole kernel corn
  ³/₄ cup water
    1 packet (1.25 ounces) ORTEGA® Taco Seasoning Mix
    1 pound linguine pasta
  ¹/₂ cup shredded Cheddar cheese

Cook and stir beef and onion in large skillet until beef is browned and onions are tender.

Stir in salsa, corn, water and seasoning mix. Cook and stir over medium heat until thickened.

Cook pasta according to package directions. Toss cooked pasta with meat mixture and top with cheese. *Makes 4 to 6 servings*

Prep Time: 5 minutes
Start-to-Finish Time: 15 minutes

Mediterranean Beef Skillet

 2¹/₂ cups (about 8 ounces) uncooked whole wheat rotini pasta
    1 pound ground beef
  ¹/₂ teaspoon dried basil
  ¹/₂ teaspoon black pepper
    1 can (about 14 ounces) diced tomatoes with garlic and onion
    1 can (8 ounces) tomato sauce
    1 bag (about 7 ounces) baby spinach, coarsely chopped
    1 can (about 2 ounces) sliced black olives, drained
  ¹/₂ cup crumbled herb-flavored feta cheese

1. Prepare pasta according to package directions; drain. Cover and keep warm.

2. Meanwhile, brown beef in large skillet over medium-high heat 6 to 8 minutes, stirring to break up meat. Drain fat. Stir in basil and pepper.

3. Reduce heat to medium. Stir in tomatoes, tomato sauce, spinach and olives; cook 10 minutes. Stir in pasta; cook 5 minutes or until heated through. Sprinkle with cheese.
Makes 4 servings

Five-Spice Beef Stir-Fry

1 boneless beef top sirloin steak (about 1 pound)
2 tablespoons soy sauce
2 tablespoons plus 1½ teaspoons cornstarch, divided
3 tablespoons walnut or vegetable oil, divided
4 carrots, cut into matchstick-size pieces (about 2 cups)
3 cups hot cooked rice
1 red bell pepper, cut into 1-inch pieces
1 yellow bell pepper, cut into 1-inch pieces
1 cup chopped onion
¼ to ½ teaspoon red pepper flakes
1½ cups water
1 tablespoon plus 1½ teaspoons packed dark brown sugar
2 teaspoons beef bouillon granules
1 teaspoon Chinese five-spice powder*
½ cup honey-roasted peanuts

Chinese five-spice powder is a blend of cinnamon, cloves, fennel seed, anise and Szechuan peppercorns. It is available in most supermarkets and at Asian grocery stores.

1. Cut steak in half lengthwise, then cut crosswise into thin strips; place in shallow baking dish. Stir soy sauce into 2 tablespoons cornstarch in small bowl until smooth. Pour soy sauce mixture over beef; toss to coat.

2. Heat 1 tablespoon oil in large nonstick skillet or wok over high heat 1 minute. Add carrots; stir-fry 3 to 4 minutes or until edges begin to brown. Combine carrots and rice in medium bowl; toss well. Cover and keep warm.

3. Reduce heat to medium-high. Add 1 tablespoon oil, bell peppers, onion and red pepper flakes; stir-fry 4 minutes or until onion is translucent. Transfer mixture to large bowl. Add remaining 1 tablespoon oil to skillet. Add half of beef; stir-fry 2 minutes or until beef is barely pink in center. Add beef to bell pepper mixture. Repeat with remaining beef.

4. Combine water, brown sugar, bouillon, five-spice powder and remaining 1½ teaspoons cornstarch in small bowl; stir until smooth. Add bouillon mixture and beef mixture to skillet; bring to a boil. Cook and stir 2 to 3 minutes or until sauce is slightly thickened. Serve beef mixture over rice; sprinkle with peanuts. *Makes 4 servings*

All-in-One Burger Stew

1 pound ground beef
2 cups frozen Italian-style vegetables
1 can (about 14 ounces) diced tomatoes with basil and garlic
1 can (about 14 ounces) beef broth
2$\frac{1}{2}$ cups uncooked medium egg noodles
Salt and black pepper

1. Brown beef in Dutch oven or large skillet over medium-high heat 6 to 8 minutes, stirring to break up meat. Drain fat.

2. Add vegetables, tomatoes and broth; bring to a boil over high heat.

3. Add noodles; reduce heat to medium. Cover; cook 12 to 15 minutes or until noodles and vegetables are tender. Season with salt and pepper. *Makes 4 to 6 servings*

Tip: To complete this meal, serve with breadsticks or a loaf of Italian bread and a salad.

Easy Beef Goulash

1 tablespoon butter
1 onion, chopped
$\frac{1}{4}$ teaspoon black pepper
1$\frac{1}{4}$ cups water
2 cups uncooked medium egg noodles
1 package (about 17 ounces) refrigerated fully cooked beef tips in gravy
1 cup frozen diced carrots and peas
1 can (4 ounces) sliced mushrooms, drained
$\frac{1}{4}$ cup red wine (optional)
$\frac{1}{3}$ cup sour cream

1. Melt butter in large skillet over medium-high heat. Add onion and pepper; cook and stir 5 minutes or until onion is translucent.

2. Add water; bring to a boil. Stir in noodles. Reduce heat to medium-low; cover and simmer 5 minutes. Stir in beef with gravy, carrots and peas, mushrooms and wine, if desired. Simmer, covered, 5 to 6 minutes or until heated through, stirring occasionally. Remove from heat. Stir in sour cream. Serve immediately. *Makes 4 servings*

All-in-One Burger Stew

Beef and Broccoli Stir-Fry

2 cups MINUTE® Brown Rice, uncooked

1 pound beef flank steak, cut into strips

2 teaspoons cornstarch

¼ cup orange juice

1 teaspoon ground ginger

1 tablespoon vegetable oil

1 package (10 ounces) frozen broccoli florets, thawed

1 can (8 ounces) sliced water chestnuts, drained

¼ cup reduced-sodium soy sauce

¼ cup dry-roasted peanuts (optional)

Prepare rice according to package directions.

Place steak strips in medium bowl. Sprinkle with cornstarch; toss to coat. Add orange juice and ginger; stir until well blended.

Heat oil in large nonstick skillet over medium-high heat. Add steak mixture; stir-fry 4 to 5 minutes or until steak is cooked through. Reduce heat to medium-low.

Add broccoli, water chestnuts and soy sauce; mix well. Cover; simmer 5 minutes or until thickened, stirring frequently. Serve over rice; sprinkle with peanuts, if desired.

Makes 4 servings

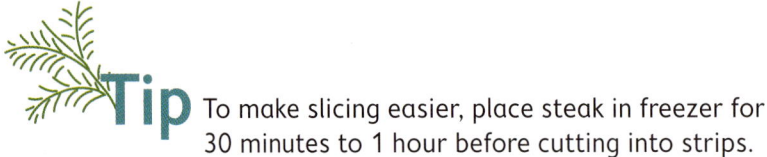

Tip To make slicing easier, place steak in freezer for 30 minutes to 1 hour before cutting into strips.

Skillet Beef and Noodles

   1 beef top sirloin steak
   1 can (10¾ ounces) condensed cream of mushroom soup, undiluted
 ¾ cup milk
 ½ cup sour cream
 ½ teaspoon salt
 ½ teaspoon black pepper
   1 tablespoon butter
   1 can (about 14 ounces) pearl onions, drained *or* 2 cups thinly sliced onions
   1 clove garlic, minced
   1 teaspoon sugar
   1 tablespoon white wine vinegar
1½ cups sliced mushrooms
   4 cups hot cooked egg noodles
   1 tablespoon minced fresh Italian parsley (optional)

1. Cut beef lengthwise in half, then crosswise into thin strips. Combine soup, milk, sour cream, salt and pepper in small bowl; mix well.

2. Melt butter in large nonstick skillet over medium heat. Add onions and garlic; cook and stir until light brown. Add sugar; cook until golden brown, stirring constantly. Stir in vinegar; cook 1 minute. Transfer to medium bowl.

3. Add mushrooms to same skillet; cook and stir until light brown. Transfer to same bowl. Increase heat to high. Add beef; stir-fry until browned. Transfer to same bowl; drain fat.

4. Add soup mixture to same skillet; cook over low heat until heated through. Stir in onions, mushrooms and beef; cook 2 minutes. (Do not boil.) Serve over noodles. Garnish with parsley.

Makes 4 servings

Southwest Skillet

3/4 pound ground beef
1 tablespoon chili powder
1 can (10 3/4 ounces) CAMPBELL'S® Condensed Beefy Mushroom Soup
1 can (14 1/2 ounces) whole peeled tomatoes, cut up
1 can (about 15 ounces) kidney beans, rinsed and drained
1/4 cup water
3/4 cup uncooked instant rice
1/2 cup shredded Cheddar cheese (2 ounces)
   Crumbled tortilla chips

1. Cook the beef with chili powder in a 10-inch skillet over medium-high heat until the beef is well browned, stirring frequently to separate meat. Pour off any fat.

2. Stir the soup, tomatoes, beans and water into the skillet. Heat to a boil. Reduce the heat to low. Cover and cook for 10 minutes.

3. Stir the rice into the skillet. Cover the skillet and remove from the heat. Let stand for 5 minutes. Top with the cheese. Serve with the chips. *Makes 4 servings*

Teriyaki Steak and Brown Rice Dinner

1 tablespoon vegetable oil
1 pound boneless beef sirloin steak, cut into strips*
1 teaspoon garlic powder
2 cups water
1/3 cup teriyaki sauce**
2 cups MINUTE® Brown Rice, uncooked
4 cups broccoli florets
1 large red bell pepper, cut into strips

Or substitute 1 pound boneless skinless chicken breasts, cut into strips.
**Or substitute 1/4 cup soy sauce plus 2 tablespoons water.*

Heat oil in large nonstick skillet over medium-high heat. Sprinkle steak with garlic powder; add to skillet; cook and stir 5 minutes or until steak is cooked through.

Stir in water and teriyaki sauce; bring to a boil. Stir in rice, broccoli and bell pepper. Return to a boil. Reduce heat to low; cover. Simmer 5 minutes. Remove from heat. Let stand 5 minutes. Fluff with fork. *Makes 4 servings*

Beef with Snow Peas & Baby Corn

  1 pound ground beef
  1 clove garlic, minced
  1 teaspoon vegetable oil
  6 ounces snow peas, halved lengthwise
  1 red bell pepper, cut into strips
  1 can (15 ounces) baby corn, drained
  1 tablespoon soy sauce
  1 teaspoon dark sesame oil
    Salt and black pepper
  2 cups cooked rice

1. Brown beef in large skillet or wok over medium-high heat 6 to 8 minutes, stirring to break up meat. Drain fat. Add garlic; cook until tender. Transfer to medium bowl.

2. Heat vegetable oil in same skillet over medium-high heat. Add snow peas and bell pepper; stir-fry 2 to 3 minutes or until vegetables are crisp-tender. Stir in beef mixture, baby corn, soy sauce and sesame oil; cook until heated through. Season with salt and black pepper. Serve over rice.

Makes 4 servings

Corned Beef Hash

  2 large russet potatoes, peeled and cut into $\frac{1}{2}$-inch cubes
  $\frac{1}{2}$ teaspoon salt
  $\frac{1}{4}$ teaspoon black pepper
  $\frac{1}{4}$ cup ($\frac{1}{2}$ stick) butter
  1 cup chopped onion
  $\frac{1}{2}$ pound corned beef, finely chopped
  1 tablespoon prepared horseradish
  4 poached or fried eggs

1. Place potatoes in 10-inch skillet. Cover potatoes with water. Bring to a boil over high heat. Reduce heat to low; simmer 6 minutes. (Potatoes will be firm.) Drain well; sprinkle potatoes with salt and pepper.

continued on page 276

Beef with Snow Peas & Baby Corn

Corned Beef Hash, continued

2. Melt butter in same skillet over medium heat. Add onion; cook and stir 5 minutes. Stir in corned beef, horseradish and potatoes; mix well. Press down mixture with spatula to flatten.

3. Reduce heat to low. Cook 10 to 15 minutes. Turn mixture in large pieces; pat down and cook 10 to 15 minutes or until bottom is well browned. Top each serving with 1 egg. Serve immediately.

Makes 4 servings

Herbed Beef & Vegetable Skillet

2 tablespoons vegetable or canola oil
1 pound boneless beef sirloin or top round steak, ³/₄-inch thick, cut into thin strips
3 medium carrots, sliced thin diagonally (about 1¹/₂ cups)
1 medium onion, chopped (about ¹/₂ cup)
2 cloves garlic, minced
¹/₂ teaspoon dried thyme leaves, crushed
1 can (10³/₄ ounces) CAMPBELL'S® Condensed Golden Mushroom Soup
¹/₄ cup water
2 teaspoons Worcestershire sauce
¹/₈ teaspoon ground black pepper
Hot cooked noodles

1. Heat **1 tablespoon** of the oil in a 12-inch skillet over medium-high heat. Add the beef and cook and stir until it's well browned. Remove the beef with a slotted spoon and set it aside.

2. Reduce the heat to medium and add the remaining oil. Add the carrots, onion, garlic and thyme. Cook and stir until the vegetables are tender-crisp.

3. Stir the soup, water, Worcestershire and black pepper into the skillet. Heat to a boil. Return the beef to the skillet and cook until the mixture is hot and bubbling. Serve over the noodles.

Makes 4 servings

Prep Time: 10 minutes
Cook Time: 20 minutes

ALL THINGS PORK

Penne with Sausage and Feta

  6 ounces uncooked penne or rigatoni pasta
    Nonstick cooking spray
12 ounces bulk mild Italian sausage
1/4 teaspoon red pepper flakes
  2 cups packed baby spinach leaves or spring greens
1/2 cup roasted red peppers, cut into thin strips
24 pitted kalamata olives, coarsely chopped
1/4 cup chopped fresh basil
  2 tablespoons extra virgin olive oil
  1 cup (4 ounces) crumbled feta cheese with tomatoes and basil
1/4 teaspoon salt

1. Cook penne according to package directions. Drain well; cover and keep warm.

2. Meanwhile, coat large skillet with cooking spray; heat over medium-high heat. Add sausage and red pepper flakes. Cook and stir until sausage is cooked through, stirring to break up meat. Drain fat.

3. Add penne, spinach, roasted peppers, olives, basil and oil to sausage mixture. Gently toss until spinach has wilted slightly. Stir in feta and salt. *Makes 4 servings*

Note: If bulk mild Italian sausage is not available, purchase regular mild Italian sausage links and remove casings prior to cooking.

Better-Than-Take-Out Fried Rice

              3 tablespoons soy sauce
              1 tablespoon rice vinegar
        ⅛ teaspoon red pepper flakes
              1 red bell pepper
              1 tablespoon peanut or vegetable oil
              6 green onions, cut into 1-inch pieces
              1 tablespoon grated fresh ginger
        1½ teaspoons minced garlic
         ½ pound boneless pork loin or tenderloin, cut into 1-inch pieces
              2 cups shredded cabbage or coleslaw mix
              1 package (8½ ounces) cooked whole grain brown rice

1. Combine soy sauce, vinegar and red pepper flakes in small bowl; mix well.

2. Cut bell pepper into decorative shapes using 1¼- to 1½-inch cookie cutters or cut into 1-inch pieces.

3. Heat oil in large nonstick skillet or wok over medium-high heat. Add bell pepper, green onions, ginger and garlic; stir-fry 1 minute. Add pork; stir-fry 2 to 3 minutes or until pork is barely pink in center.

4. Stir in cabbage, rice and soy sauce mixture; cook and stir 1 minute or until heated through.

Makes 4 servings

Prep Time: 15 minutes

Ham and Sweet Potato Skillet

  2 sweet potatoes (about 1¼ pounds)
  3 cups water
  1 tablespoon salt
  1 fully cooked ham steak (about 1 pound)
  ½ cup brewed coffee
  ¼ cup pure maple syrup
  2 tablespoons butter
  ½ cup coarsely chopped pecans, toasted

1. Peel sweet potatoes; cut into ¾-inch pieces. Combine water and salt in large saucepan over medium heat. Add sweet potatoes; simmer 8 to 10 minutes or until almost tender. Drain well.

2. Meanwhile, cut ham into ¾-inch chunks; discard bone and fat. Set aside.

3. Combine coffee, maple syrup and butter in large skillet. Bring to a boil over high heat. Reduce heat to medium-low; simmer 3 minutes. Add ham and sweet potatoes; simmer until ham is heated through and sauce is bubbly and slightly thickened, stirring occasionally. Sprinkle with pecans just before serving.   *Makes 4 servings*

Rosemary Pork Chops

  1 tablespoon vegetable oil
  4 pork chops
  1 small onion, chopped
  2 cups MINUTE® White Rice, uncooked
  1 cup roasted red peppers, drained, chopped
  1 can (14½ ounces) beef broth
  ¼ cup balsamic vinaigrette dressing
  ½ teaspoon dried rosemary

Heat oil in large nonstick skillet over medium-high heat. Add chops; cook 6 minutes or until cooked through (160°F), turning after 3 minutes. Remove from skillet; cover to keep warm.

Add onions to skillet. Cook 5 minutes or until onions are tender, stirring occasionally.

Stir in rice, peppers, broth, dressing and rosemary. Bring to a boil. Reduce heat to medium-low; simmer 5 minutes. Serve chops with rice.   *Makes 4 servings*

Ham and Sweet Potato Skillet

Hearty Sausage & Rice Skillet

       1 pound bulk pork sausage
       1 package (8 ounces) sliced mushrooms
       2 stalks celery, coarsely chopped
       1 large red pepper, coarsely chopped
       1 large onion, coarsely chopped (about 1 cup)
       1 teaspoon dried thyme leaves, crushed
     ½ teaspoon dried marjoram leaves, crushed
  1¾ cups SWANSON® Chicken Broth (Regular, Natural Goodness® or Certified Organic)
       1 can (10¾ ounces) CAMPBELL'S® Condensed Cream of Mushroom Soup (Regular or
           98% Fat Free)
       1 box (6 ounces) long-grain white and wild rice blend
       1 cup shredded Cheddar cheese (4 ounces)

1. Cook the sausage in a 12-inch oven-safe skillet over medium-high heat until the sausage is well browned, stirring frequently to separate meat. Pour off any fat.

2. Add the mushrooms, celery, pepper, onion, thyme, marjoram and seasoning packet from the rice blend and cook until the vegetables are tender-crisp. Stir in the broth, soup, rice blend and ½ **cup** of the cheese. **Cover.**

3. Bake at 375°F. for 1 hour or until hot and bubbly and the rice is tender. Uncover and stir. Sprinkle with the remaining cheese.   *Makes 6 servings*

Prep Time: 15 minutes
Bake Time: 1 hour

Teriyaki Rib Dinner

1 package (about 15 ounces) refrigerated fully cooked pork baby back ribs
in barbecue sauce
2 tablespoons vegetable oil
1 onion, thinly sliced
4 cups frozen stir-fry vegetables
1 can (8 ounces) pineapple chunks, undrained *or* 1 cup diced fresh pineapple
¼ cup hoisin sauce
2 tablespoons cider vinegar

1. Remove ribs from package; reserve barbecue sauce. Cut into individual ribs; set aside.

2. Heat oil in Dutch oven over medium-high heat. Add onion; cook 3 minutes or until translucent. Add vegetables; cook and stir 4 minutes.

3. Add ribs, reserved sauce, pineapple, hoisin sauce and vinegar; mix well. Cover; cook 5 minutes or until heated through.

Makes 4 servings

Spanish Rice with Chorizo

4 links Spanish-style chorizo sausage (about 12 ounces)
1 green bell pepper, diced
1½ cups uncooked instant rice
1 can (about 14 ounces) diced tomatoes
1 cup chicken broth or water
2 green onions, chopped
Salt and black pepper

1. Thinly slice sausage on the diagonal. Cook sausage and bell pepper in large nonstick skillet over medium heat 5 minutes or until bell pepper is tender, stirring frequently. Stir in rice, tomatoes, broth and green onions.

2. Increase heat to high. Bring to boil. Reduce heat to medium-low; cover and simmer 8 to 10 minutes or until liquid is absorbed and rice is tender. Season with salt and black pepper.

Makes 4 servings

Note: For a vegetarian version, substitute soy-based sausages for the chorizo. Use 1 tablespoon vegetable oil in skillet with sausages and bell pepper. Substitute vegetable broth or water for the chicken broth.

Teriyaki Rib Dinner

Skillet Pasta Roma

$\frac{1}{2}$ pound Italian sausage, sliced or crumbled
1 large onion, coarsely chopped
1 large clove garlic, minced
2 cans (14$\frac{1}{2}$ ounces each) DEL MONTE® Diced Tomatoes with Basil, Garlic & Oregano
1 can (8 ounces) DEL MONTE Tomato Sauce
1 cup water
8 ounces uncooked rotini or other spiral pasta
8 mushrooms, sliced (optional)
Grated Parmesan cheese and fresh thyme sprigs (optional)

1. Brown sausage in large skillet. Add onion and garlic. Cook until onion is soft; drain. Stir in undrained tomatoes, tomato sauce, water and pasta.

2. Cover and bring to a boil; reduce heat. Simmer, covered, 25 to 30 minutes or until pasta is tender, stirring occasionally.

3. Stir in mushrooms, if desired; simmer 5 minutes. Serve in skillet garnished with cheese and thyme, if desired.

Makes 4 servings

**Tip** Skillet dishes are a fast and easy way to put dinner on the table every night. They require just a few ingredients and use only one pan. This makes cleanup a breeze and leaves you with plenty of time to enjoy a tasty meal with family or friends.

Sweet and Sour Pork

1 tablespoon soy sauce
2 cloves garlic, minced
1 pound boneless pork loin or tenderloin
1 can (8 ounces) pineapple chunks in juice, undrained
2 tablespoons peanut or vegetable oil, divided
2 carrots, cut diagonally into thin slices
1 green bell pepper, cut into 1-inch pieces
⅓ cup stir-fry sauce
1 tablespoon white wine or white vinegar
   Hot cooked rice

1. Combine soy sauce and garlic in medium bowl. Cut pork into 1-inch pieces; toss with soy sauce mixture. Drain pineapple, reserving 2 tablespoons juice.

2. Heat large skillet or wok over medium-high heat 1 minute. Add 1 tablespoon oil; heat 30 seconds. Add pork mixture; stir-fry 4 to 5 minutes or until pork is barely pink in center. Transfer to plate.

3. Heat remaining 1 tablespoon oil in same skillet. Add carrots and bell pepper; stir-fry 4 to 5 minutes or until vegetables are crisp-tender. Add pineapple; stir-fry until heated through.

4. Add stir-fry sauce, reserved pineapple juice and vinegar; stir-fry 30 seconds or until sauce comes to a boil. Return pork along with any accumulated juices to skillet; cook and stir until heated through. Serve over rice. *Makes 4 servings*

Pork Chop Skillet Dinner

    1 tablespoon olive oil or vegetable oil
    4 bone-in pork chops, 3/4-inch thick
    1 medium onion, chopped (about 1/2 cup)
    1 cup uncooked regular long-grain white rice
    1 can (10 1/2 ounces) CAMPBELL'S® Condensed Chicken Broth
    1 cup orange juice
    3 tablespoons chopped fresh parsley
    4 orange slices

1. Heat the oil in a 10-inch skillet over medium-high heat. Add the pork and cook until it's well browned on both sides.

2. Add the onion and rice to the skillet and cook and stir until the rice is browned. Stir in the broth, orange juice and **2 tablespoons** parsley and heat to a boil. Reduce the heat to low. Cover and cook for 20 minutes or until the pork is cooked through and the rice is tender.

3. Top with the orange slices and sprinkle with the remaining parsley.   *Makes 4 servings*

Southern Pork Barbecue Dinner

     1 tablespoon vegetable oil
    1/2 cup chopped onion
    1/2 cup chopped celery
    1/2 cup chopped green bell pepper
     1 container (about 18 ounces) refrigerated fully cooked shredded pork
     1 can (about 15 ounces) pinto beans or black-eyed peas, rinsed and drained
     1 can (8 ounces) tomato sauce
     2 tablespoons Dijon mustard

1. Heat oil in large skillet over medium-high heat. Add onion, celery and bell pepper; cook and stir 5 minutes or until tender.

2. Reduce heat to low. Stir in pork, beans, tomato sauce and mustard; cook 10 minutes or until heated through.   *Makes 4 to 6 servings*

Mozzarella-Pepper Sausage Skillet

 1 pound mild Italian sausage, casings removed
 1 tablespoon olive oil
 1 package (8 ounces) sliced mushrooms
 1 zucchini, thinly sliced
 ¾ cup finely chopped onion
 1 tablespoon dried basil
 1 can (8 ounces) tomato sauce
 ½ cup plain dry bread crumbs
 ¼ teaspoon salt
 1 red bell pepper, cut into strips
 1 green bell pepper, cut into strips
 1½ cups (6 ounces) shredded mozzarella cheese

1. Brown sausage in large nonstick skillet 6 to 8 minutes over medium-high heat, stirring to break up meat. Drain fat; transfer sausage to plate.

2. Add oil to same skillet. Add mushrooms, zucchini, onion and basil; cook and stir 5 minutes or until zucchini is tender.

3. Return sausage to skillet. Add tomato sauce, bread crumbs and salt; mix well. Top mixture with bell peppers. Cover; simmer 25 minutes or until bell peppers are tender. Remove from heat. Sprinkle with cheese. Cover; let stand until cheese is melted.   *Makes 4 servings*

So Easy Seafood

Spicy Crabmeat Frittata

   1 tablespoon olive oil
   1 green bell pepper, finely chopped
   2 cloves garlic, minced
   6 eggs
   1 can (6½ ounces) lump white crabmeat, drained
 ¼ teaspoon black pepper
 ¼ teaspoon salt
 ¼ teaspoon hot pepper sauce
   1 plum tomato, seeded and finely chopped

1. Preheat broiler. Heat oil in large ovenproof skillet over medium-high heat. Add bell pepper and garlic; cook and stir 3 minutes or until tender.

2. Meanwhile, beat eggs in medium bowl. Break up large pieces of crabmeat. Add crabmeat, black pepper, salt and hot pepper sauce to eggs; stir gently until well blended.

3. Add tomato to skillet; cook and stir 1 minute. Stir in egg mixture. Reduce heat to medium-low; cook 7 minutes or until eggs begin to set around edges.

4. Transfer skillet to broiler. Broil 2 minutes or until center is set and top is browned. Serve immediately. *Makes 4 servings*

Cheesy Tuna Dinner

    1 can (10¾ ounces) condensed cream of mushroom soup
1½ cups milk
    2 cans (6 ounces each) tuna, drained, flaked
    1 cup frozen green peas, thawed
    2 cups MINUTE® White Rice, uncooked
    1 cup Cheddar cheese, shredded
      Canned French-fried onions or crushed potato chips (optional)

Mix soup and milk in medium saucepan. Bring to a boil over medium heat, stirring frequently.

Add tuna and peas; mix well. Return to a boil.

Stir in rice and cheese; cover. Reduce heat to low; cook 5 minutes. Stir until cheese is melted. Garnish with onions or chips, if desired.   *Makes 4 servings*

Cajun-Style Corn with Crayfish

    6 ears of corn
    1 tablespoon vegetable oil
    1 onion, chopped
½ cup chopped green bell pepper
½ cup chopped red bell pepper
    1 cup water
    1 teaspoon salt
⅛ teaspoon black pepper
⅛ teaspoon ground red pepper
¾ pound crayfish tail meat

1. Cut corn from cobs in two or three layers so that kernels are not left whole. Scrape cobs to remove remaining juice and pulp.

2. Heat oil in large skillet over medium heat. Add onion and bell peppers; cook 5 minutes, stirring occasionally. Add corn, water, salt, black pepper and ground red pepper; bring to a boil. Reduce heat to low; simmer 10 to 15 minutes.

3. Add crayfish; simmer 3 to 5 minutes or just until crayfish turn opaque. Serve immediately.   *Makes 6 servings*

Cheesy Tuna Dinner

Noodles with Baby Shrimp

1 package (3¾ ounces) bean thread noodles
3 green onions
1 tablespoon vegetable oil
1 package (16 ounces) frozen stir-fry vegetables
1 cup vegetable broth
8 ounces cooked frozen baby shrimp
1 tablespoon soy sauce
2 teaspoons dark sesame oil
¼ teaspoon black pepper

1. Place noodles in large bowl. Cover with warm water; let stand 10 to 15 minutes or just until softened. Drain noodles. Cut noodles into 5- to 6-inch pieces; set aside. Cut green onions into 1-inch pieces.

2. Heat large skillet or wok over high heat 1 minute. Add vegetable oil; heat 30 seconds. Add green onions; stir-fry 1 minute. Add vegetables; stir-fry 2 minutes. Add broth; bring to a boil. Reduce heat to low; cover and simmer 5 minutes or until vegetables are crisp-tender.

3. Add shrimp; cook just until thawed. Stir in noodles, soy sauce, sesame oil and pepper; stir-fry until heated through.   *Makes 4 to 6 servings*

Mango Catfish Couscous

Nonstick cooking spray
12 ounces catfish fillets, cut into 2-inch pieces
1 ripe mango, sliced lengthwise and peeled
2 zucchini, cubed
2 yellow squash, cubed
1 red bell pepper, chopped
1 cup orange juice
¾ cup vegetable broth
½ cup sliced green onions
1 teaspoon dried parsley flakes
¼ teaspoon paprika
¼ teaspoon white pepper
Hot cooked couscous

Lightly coat large skillet with cooking spray; heat over medium-high heat. Add catfish, mango, zucchini, squash, bell pepper, juice, broth, green onions, parsley, paprika and white pepper. Cook 30 minutes, stirring occasionally. Serve over couscous. *Makes 4 servings*

Poached Salmon & Asparagus

2 tablespoons butter
1 cup onion, sliced
2 stalks celery, sliced
1 cup asparagus stems, sliced
2 packages UNCLE BEN'S® NATURAL SELECT® Garlic & Butter Flavor Rice
3 cups water
6 pieces salmon fillets
1 cup asparagus tips

1. In large skillet with tight-fitting lid, melt butter over medium heat and sauté onion, celery and asparagus stems for about 3 minutes.

2. Add rice and water; bring to a boil. Carefully place fillets on top of rice; reduce heat. Cover and simmer about 4 minutes.

3. Arrange asparagus tips around salmon fillets; cover and simmer 6 to 8 minutes longer.
Makes 6 servings

Southwestern Tilapia with Rice and Beans

2 tablespoons all-purpose flour
¼ teaspoon salt, divided
⅛ teaspoon black pepper
4 tilapia fillets, patted dry
2 tablespoons butter, divided
1 package (about 8 ounces) ready-to-serve Spanish rice
1 can (about 14 ounces) diced tomatoes with chiles or chipotle chiles
1 can (about 15 ounces) black beans, rinsed and drained
¼ teaspoon crushed dried oregano
1 green onion, finely chopped

1. Combine flour, ⅛ teaspoon salt and pepper in a gallon-size resealable food storage bag. Add tilapia and shake to coat.

2. Melt 1 tablespoon butter in large skillet over medium-high heat. Add tilapia; cook 4 minutes or until golden brown and fish just begins to flake when tested with fork, turning once. Transfer to plate; keep warm.

3. Add remaining 1 tablespoon butter to same skillet. Add rice and separate grains with a fork. Stir in tomatoes, black beans, oregano and remaining ⅛ teaspoon salt. Reduce heat to low; simmer 5 minutes, stirring frequently. Sprinkle with green onion. Serve tilapia with rice mixture. *Makes 4 servings*

**Tip** Because fish overcooks quickly, watch it closely while cooking. When the fish is done, it feels slightly springy, looks opaque and has lost all its translucency. Don't wait until it flakes easily or the fish will be dry.

Gingered Shrimp and Vegetable Fried Rice Skillet

Nonstick cooking spray
½ pound large raw shrimp, peeled and deveined
2 teaspoons minced fresh ginger
3 cloves garlic, minced
2 cups snow peas
1 red or yellow bell pepper, cut into thin 1-inch strips
3 tablespoons soy sauce
1 package (8½ ounces) cooked brown rice
1 tablespoon dark sesame oil
¼ cup chopped fresh cilantro or green onions

1. Spray large nonstick skillet with cooking spray; heat over medium-high heat. Add shrimp, ginger and garlic; stir-fry 1 minute.

2. Add snow peas and bell pepper; stir-fry 4 minutes or until shrimp are pink and opaque and vegetables are crisp-tender. Stir in soy sauce; stir-fry 1 minute.

3. Add rice; stir-fry 2 minutes or until heated through. Remove from heat; stir in sesame oil and cilantro.

Makes 2 to 4 servings

Creole Shrimp and Rice

2 tablespoons olive oil
1 cup uncooked white rice
1 can (about 14 ounces) diced tomatoes with garlic
1½ cups water
1 teaspoon Creole or Cajun seasoning
1 pound peeled cooked medium shrimp
1 package (10 ounces) frozen okra *or* 1½ cups frozen sugar snap peas, thawed

1. Heat oil in large skillet over medium heat. Add rice; cook and stir 2 to 3 minutes or until lightly browned.

2. Add tomatoes, water and seasoning; bring to a boil. Reduce heat to medium-low; cover and simmer 15 minutes. Add shrimp and okra; simmer, covered, 3 minutes or until heated through.

Makes 4 servings

Prep and Cook Time: 20 minutes

Halibut Provençale

Nonstick cooking spray
1 can (28 ounces) diced tomatoes
2 cups fennel, stems and fronds removed, sliced thin and chopped
1 cup finely chopped onion
2 tablespoons minced orange peel
2 teaspoons herbes de Provence
4 (4-ounce) halibut steaks (½ inch thick)
1 tablespoon olive oil
¼ cup plain dry bread crumbs
1 tablespoon grated Parmesan cheese
2 cloves garlic, minced
1 teaspoon paprika
½ teaspoon black pepper
¼ teaspoon salt
Minced fresh basil (optional)

1. Spray 12-inch skillet with cooking spray; heat over medium heat. Add tomatoes, fennel, onion, orange peel and herbes de Provence. Cook and stir 10 minutes.

2. Place halibut over vegetables; drizzle with oil. Combine bread crumbs, cheese, garlic, paprika, pepper and salt in small bowl. Sprinkle over fish. Cover; cook 5 to 6 minutes or until fish just begins to flake when tested with fork. Garnish with basil.   *Makes 4 servings*

Note: Herbes de Provence spice mixes usually contain dried basil, fennel seed, lavender, marjoram, rosemary, sage, summer savory and thyme.

Smoked Salmon Hash Browns

        3 cups frozen hash brown potatoes, thawed
        2 pouches (3 ounces each) smoked salmon*
    ½ cup chopped onion
    ½ cup chopped green bell pepper
    ¼ teaspoon black pepper
        2 tablespoons vegetable oil

Smoked salmon in foil pouches can be found in the canned fish section of the supermarket. Do not substitute lox or other fresh smoked salmon.

1. Combine potatoes, salmon, onion, bell pepper and black pepper in large bowl; mix well.

2. Heat oil in large skillet over medium-high heat. Add potato mixture; pat down evenly.

3. Cook 5 minutes or until bottom is crisp and brown. Turn over in large pieces. Cook 2 to 3 minutes or until both sides are browned.   *Makes 4 servings*

Easy Halibut Steaks with Tomato and Broccoli Sauce

        2 tablespoons olive oil
        2 cups chopped broccoli
  2½ cups diced tomatoes
        2 tablespoons lemon juice
        1 tablespoon chopped garlic
        1 tablespoon fresh tarragon *or* 1 teaspoon dried tarragon
    ½ teaspoon sugar
    ½ teaspoon salt
    ½ teaspoon black pepper
        4 halibut steaks (4 ounces each)

1. Heat oil in large skillet over medium heat. Add broccoli; cook 5 minutes.

2. Add tomatoes, lemon juice, garlic, tarragon, sugar, salt and pepper; cook 5 minutes, stirring occasionally.

3. Add halibut; cover and cook 10 minutes or until fish is opaque, turning once.
                                                                     Makes 4 servings

Smoked Salmon Hash Browns

The publisher would like to thank the companies and organizations listed below for the use of their recipes and photographs in this publication.

Campbell Soup Company

ConAgra Foods, Inc.

Del Monte Foods

Florida Department of Agriculture and Consumer Services, Bureau of Seafood and Aquaculture

ConAgra Foods, Inc.

Hillshire Farm®

Idaho Potato Commission

Jennie-O Turkey Store, LLC

®Johnsonville Sausage, LLC

Kraft Foods Global, Inc.

MASTERFOODS USA

Michael Foods, Inc.

National Fisheries Institute

National Turkey Federation

Norseland, Inc.

Ortega®, A Division of B&G Foods, Inc.

Reckitt Benckiser Inc.

Riviana Foods Inc.

Sargento® Foods Inc.

Tyson Foods, Inc.

Unilever

Veg•All®